1 MONTH OF
FREE
READING

at
www.ForgottenBooks.com

By purchasing this book you are eligible for one month membership to ForgottenBooks.com, giving you unlimited access to our entire collection of over 1,000,000 titles via our web site and mobile apps.

To claim your free month visit:
www.forgottenbooks.com/free871098

ISBN 978-0-266-58571-8
PIBN 10871098

A

SPELLING-BOOK,

CONTAINING

THE RUDIMENTS

ÓF THE

ENGLISH LANGUAGE;

WITH

APPROPRIATE READING LESSONS.

By THOMAS J. LEE, Esq.

SECOND EDITION.

BOSTON :

PUBLISHED BY MUNROE AND FRANCIS,

NO. 4, CORNHILL.

1823.

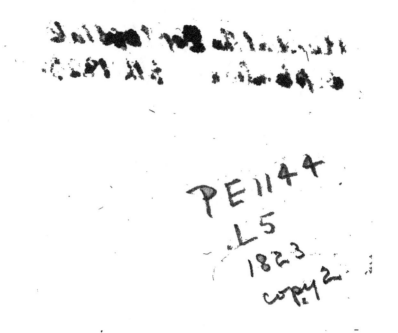

DISTRICT OF MASSACHUSETTS, TO WIT:

District Clerk's Office.

L. S. Be it remembered, that on the eighth day of May, A.D. 1823, in the forty-seventh year of the Independence of the United States of America, THOMAS J. LEE, Esq. of the said District, has deposited in this Office, the Title of a Book, the right whereof he claims as Author and Proprietor, in the words following, *to wit:*

A SPELLING-BOOK, containing the Rudiments of the English Language, with appropriate Reading Lessons. By Thomas J. Lee, Esq. Second Edition.

In conformity to the act of the Congress of the United States, entitled, "An act for the encouragement of learning, by securing the copies of maps, charts and books, to the authors and proprietors of such copies, during the times therein mentioned," and also to an act entitled, "An act supplementary to an act, entitled, an act for the encouragement of learning, by securing the copies of maps, charts and books, to the authors and proprietors of such copies during the times therein mentioned; and extending the benefits thereof to the arts of designing, engraving, and etching historical and other prints."

JOHN W. DAVIS, Clerk of the District of Massachusetts.

PREFACE.

Nothing is attempted in this manual but a careful selection from the mass of materials already before the public, and such an arrangement of them, as it is hoped will facilitate the progress of the learner.

The vowels are arranged in such a manner as best to answer the purpose of instruction. The number of simple vowel sounds, as given by Murray, has been chosen as containing the regular sounds of the vowels. The most common of the irregularly sounded vowels, and improper diphthongs, and such consonants and double consonants as have more than one sound, are inserted in the table of sounds.

The multitude of characters used in some Spelling-Books to designate sounds, is unnecessary and perplexing to the learner. Of what use is it, that syllables, which always have the same sound, should have characters placed over them whenever they occur? A judicious arrangement, and natural division of words, with directions for placing the accent, are generally sufficient to convey the sounds of the letters. The Compiler has endeavoured, in this book, to class the monosyllables and dissyllables (except a few easy words in the former part of the book) so as to convey the sounds accurately. But it is thought, that in words of three or more syllables, if the accented syllable be pointed out, the learner will usually pronounce the others correctly.

In the division of words into syllables, it is best to " divide them as they are naturally divided in a right pronunciation," and as is most agreeable to the ear. If, in addition to this, it is observed, that compound words should be resolved into their primitive, and grammatical terminations carefully separated in spelling, no further direction seems necessary.

It has not been the intention of the Compiler to collect complete lists of the various classes of words, which would introduce many words seldom used, and only in learned works; nor did he intend to insert uncommon words in the spelling lessons, but to collect a sufficient number of those in common use, which ought to be learned first. Such words will afford abundant exercise for the learner, and sufficient examples of the various sounds of the letters ; and recourse may always be had to dictionaries to ascertain the pronunciation of uncommon and technical terms.

The orthography of Johnson has been followed except in the omission of k in words ending with ic, as public, And the pronunciation of Walker has been followed except in the words, clerk, clerkship, cucumber, deaf, lieutenant, pour, raisin, and sergeant. Good usage in this country seems to have decided in favour of a more analogical pronunciation for these words than he has given them. Where Walker has given more than one method of pronunciation, the Compiler has made his election.

Children should be made to distinguish the various sounds of the vowels and consonants, by which they are much assisted in reading and spelling. In using this book, let them be taught the table of sounds, and be taught to pronounce the several vowel sounds, detached from the key-words in which they stand. When they become thorough and ready in this exercise, they may be directed to designate the sounds of the letters in the following manner.

Catastrophe ; hard *c*, short *a*,* short *a*, sharp *s*, long *o*, *ph* like *f*, and long *e*.

Anonymous ; short *a*, short *o*, *y* like *e* long, silent *o*, short *u*, and sharp *s*.

Chandelier ; *ch* like *sh*, short *a*, long *e*, silent *i*, and long *e*.

Parson ; *a* middle, *s* sharp, and silent *o*.

Parent ; *a* long, and short *e*.

Improve ; short *i*, middle *o*, and silent *e*.

Legible ; short *e*, soft *g*, *i* like *e* long, and silent *e*.

Decrease ; long *e*, hard *c*, *ea* like *e* long, sharp *s* and silent *e*.

In selecting the Reading Lessons, simplicity and purity have been sought, both in style and sentiment ; and a few selections from the Bible have been introduced. The arrangement, it is hoped, is such, as will advance the learner by easy gradations.

Common names of persons, and names of distinguished places, are inserted. It is apparent that

* When *a* ends an unaccented syllable, its sound is difficult to appreciate. It seems best to consider it short, as Walker has done. The final *a* should be sounded like *ah*.

1*

youth should early be made acquainted with their orthography and pronunciation.

In the 24th chapter, the first word of each couplet, may be considered as a key to the sound of the succeeding word.

The Compiler has endeavoured to put the elementary lessons into such a form as to be easily committed to memory and retained. In preparing them, he has made use of the language of other persons, whenever it met his own views.

Perhaps there is no way to express the *Abbrevia-tions* so clearly as to supersede the necessity of explanation from the teacher. Children should be taught that the same initial or abbreviation sometimes stands for different words, and the same words are represented by different abbreviations. They should also be taught *where* they are used.

The importance of examining pupils by questions relative to their studies, is manifest. Questions on some of the chapters are annexed for the purpose; which it is hoped will contribute to the ease of the instructer, and the advancement of the pupil.

A select collection of words with brief definitions is annexed to exercise the more advanced pupil in spelling and defining. A few words in which the pronunciation differs from the orthography, have the sounds pointed out by a different spelling. This list will be found to contain the principal words used in the elementary and reading lessons, and thus in a measure answer the purpose of a dictionary for the pupil.

Royalston, Mass. 1821.

THE ALPHABET.

Roman.		Italic.		Old English.		Names.
A	a	A	a	A	a	a
B	b	B	b	B	b	bee
C	c	C	c	C	c	cee
D	d	D	d	D	d	dee
E	e	E	e	E	e	e
F	f	F	f	F	f	ef
G	g	G	g	G	g	je
H	h	H	h	H	h	aitch
I	i	I	i	I	i	i *or* eye
J	j	J	j	J	j	jay
K	k	K	k	K	k	ka
L	l	L	l	L	l	el
M	m	M	m	M	m	em
N	n	N	n	N	n	en
O	o	O	o	O	o	o
P	p	P	p	P	p	pee
Q	q	Q	q	Q	q	cue
R	r	R	r	R	r	ar
S	s	S	s	S	s	ess
T	t	T	t	T	t	tee
U	u	U	u	U	u	you
V	v	V	v	V	v	vee
W	w	W	w	W	w	double u
X	x	X	x	X	x	eks
Y	y	Y	y	Y	y	wy
Z	z	Z	z	Z	z	zee

ALPHABETS.

Capital Letters.

H Q G O Z N A

R F P C S M E

J X Y D U K V

B W L T I

Small Letters.

m k j o q l p r n

i g e d a f b h c

s w u v z y t x &

Vowels.

a e i o u, and sometimes w and y.

Consonants.

b c d f g h j k l m n p q r s t v x z

Double and Triple Letters.

Æ Œ æ œ ff fi ffi fl ffl

Figures.

1 2 3 4 5 6 7 8 9 0

CHAPTER I.

Table of Sounds.

REGULAR VOWELS.

a long,	*as heard in*	hate.
a short,	. . . .	hat.
a middle,	. . . .	part.
a broad,	. . . . .	hall.
e long,	. . . . .	mete.
e short,	. . . . .	met.
i long,	. . . . .	pine.
i short,	. . . . .	pin.
o long,	. . . . .	note.
o short,	. . . . .	not.
o middle,	. . . . .	prove.
u long,	. . . . .	duke.
u short,	. . . . .	duck.
u middle,	. . . . .	bush.

IRREGULAR VOWELS.

a like o short,	*as heard in*	wash.
a like u short,	. . . .	liar.
e like u short,	. . . .	her.
i like u short,	. . . .	shirt.
i like e long,	. . . . .	caprice.
o like u short,	. . . .	done.
o like a broad,	. . . .	nor.
y like i long,	. . . .	by.
y like e long,	. . . .	beauty.

PROPER DIPHTHONGS.

oi } have the combined sound of broad a, { oil,
oy }   and long e, as heard in   { boy.
ou } have the combined sound of broad a, { our,
ov }   and middle u, as heard in   { cow.

IMPROPER DIPHTHONGS.

ai like a long, *as heard in* ail.

au like a broad, ... fault.

au like a middle, . . . aunt.

aw like a broad. . . . awl.

ay like a long, ... day.

ea like e long, ... lean.

ea like e short, ... head.

ee like e long, ... deed.

ei like a long, ... vein.

ei like e long, ... seize.

ew like u long, ... blew.

ie like e long, ... bier.

ie like i long, ... pie.

oa like o long, ... load.

oe like o long, ... hoe.

oo like o middle, . . . cool.

oo like u middle . . . good.

CONSONANTS.

c hard like k, *as heard in* cash.
c soft like s, ... cellar.
c like sh, ... ocean, special.
c like z, ... suffice.
ch hard, ... cHord.
ch soft, ... *ch*aise.
ch like tch, ... cheese.
d proper, ... death.
d soft like j, ... soldier.
g hard, ... gone.
g soft, ... gem.
gh like f, ... laugh.
ph like f, ... phlegm.
s sharp, ... saint.
s soft, ... rose.
t proper, ... take.
t like tch, ... nature.
th hard, ... thin.
th soft, ... THine.
x flat, like gz, ... exalt.
x sharp like ks, . . . extreme.

Some of the consonant sounds are denoted by small capitals and Italies ; all other Italic letters are silent. So many of the silent vowels are printed in Italics, as seemed necessary to convey the sounds of the syllables. The final e preceded by l and a mute is always silent. Where e final lengthens the syllable, it is printed in Roman letters. G is soft before *e*, *i*, and *y*,—and *i* and *y*, ending an unaccented syllable, sound like *e* long, unless otherwise noted.

CHAPTER II.

Words of Two Letters.

ab	eb	ib	ob	ub
ac	ec	ic	oc	uc
ad	ed	id	od	ud
af	ef	if	of	uf
ag	eg	ig	og	ug
al	el	il	ol	ul
am	em	im	om	um
an	en	in	on	un
ap	ep	ip	op	up
ar	er	ir	or	ur
as	es	is	os	us
at	et	it	ot	ut

~~~~~~~~~~~~~~~~~~

ba	be	bi	bo	bu	by
ca	ce	ci	co	cu	cy
da	de	di	do	du	dy
fa	fe	fi	fo	fu	fy
ga	ge	gi	go	gu	gy
ha	he	hi	ho	hu	hy
la	le	li	lo	lu	ly
ma	me	mi	mo	mu	my
na	ne	ni	no	nu	ny

pa	pe	pi	po	pu	py
ra	re	ri	ro	ru	ry
sa	se	si	so	su	sy

by	go	to	he	be
my	lo	wo	me	ye
do	so	or	we	no

ah	am	an	at	as
is	it	if	in	on
ox	of	up	us	

bla	ble	bli	blo	blu
bra	bre	bri	bro	bru
cla	cle	cli	clo	clu

add	Ann	asp	end
aft	apt	egg	ill
and	ask	ell	ink

I do so.

Is he up ?

He is up.

So am I.

Go with me.

Do as I do.

Do so to us.

Do as we do.

Do so to me.

It is my hat.

2

Vowels short.

Bad	mat	met	hip	win
bag	nag	peg	his	wit
ban	nap	pen	hit	Bog
bat	pad	pet	jig	cob
cag	pan	red	kid	cog
can	rag	ten	kin	con
cap	ran	web	lid	cot
cat	rap	wed	lip	dog
dab	rat	wet	mix	dot
fag	sap	wen	nib	fog
fan	tan	Bid	nip	fop
fat	tap	big	nit	fox
gad	tax	bin	pig	got
gag	Bed	bit	pin	hod
gap	beg	cit	pit	hog
had	bet	did	rib	hop
hag	den	dig	rid	hot
ham	fed	dim	rig	jog
hap	fen	din	rim	jot
hat	hem	dip	rip	log
lad	hen	fib	sin	lop
lag	keg	fig	sip	lot
lap	ken	fin	sit	mop
lax	led	fit	six	pod
mad	leg	fix	tin	pop
man	let	hid	tip	pot
map	men	him	wig	rob

rod	top	cut	hug	nut
rot	wot	Dug	hum	pun
sob	Bud	dun	hut	rub
sod	bug	fun	jug	rug
sog	bun	gum	jut	rum
sop	but	gun	lug	run
sot	cub	hub	mug	sum

Vowels long.

ace	ape	eke	ile	ore
age	ate	ire	ode	use
ale	eve	ice	old	THE

Is it so ?

Wo to us.

It is on me.

As I go by.

So am I in.

It is to be so.

Am I to go in ?

It is my ox.

Am I to go up ?

I am as he is.

It is my top.

Do we go to bed ?

Ann is to go.

My hat is by me.

Put it on.

Let me try.

Do not cry.

A fat hog.

A fat pig.

A bad lad.

A red hat.

A hot bit for me.

A sly fox.

Cut it up.

Cut it for me.

I try to do it.

Did Ann go ?

Get his hat.

A mad man.

The sun is up.

I can go to him.

Is he to do it ?

Am I to do it ?

An old man.

Pen and ink.

Run to me.

Vowels Short.

Band	hang	fret	stem
bank	hank	gem	tell
bang	land	held	Brim
blab	lank	help	chin
brad	mask	jest	chip
brat	mass	lend	chit
cash	pang	lent	clip
cask	plan	lest	crib
chap	plat	melt	dint
chat	rack	mend	dish
clad	rang	neck	disk
clam	sack	nest	drip
clan	sand	next	flit
crab	sank	peck	fill
crag	sang	pelf	fish
cram	sash	pelt	glib
dash	shad	pent	grin
drab	Beck	pest	grit
drag	bell	rent	hill
dram	belt	rest	hilt
fact	bend	self	hint
fang	bent	sell	kill
flag	deck	send	king
gash	desk	sent	lift
glad	fell	shed	link
hack	felt	sled	live
hand	fend	sped	mill

mint	tick	lock	slop
miss	till	loll	spot
pill	tint	loss	trod
pink	Blot	long	trot
pith	bond	mob	Buck
rich	box	mock	buff
ring	chop	moss	bulk
risk	clod	moth	bung
shin	clot	plod	club
ship	crop	plot	crum
sick	doll	pomp	cull
sing	drop	pond	curb
sink	flog	prop	curd
slid	fob	rock	curl
slim	fond	scot	drug
slit	font	shod	duck
smit	frog	shop	dull
spit	from	shot	

A mad dog.
He can dig.
I can hop.
We can run.
A red bud.
A dry fig.
Get my hat.
Let us go in.
A red spot.
A pink sash.
The left hand.

A dish of milk.
Give me a pin.
Do not hurt me.
A long pole.
A cup of tea.
Here is a bee.
A ripe plum.
A kind man.
It is a fine day.
The fire burns.
Let me see you hop.

2*

Vowels Long.

Bale	lave	save	hind
bane	mace	take	hire
bate	made	tale	kine
cage	make	tame	kite
cake	male	vale	lice
came	mane	vane	like
cane	mate	vase	life
cape	name	wade	lime
case	nape	wage	line
cave	nave	wake	mice
dale	pace	wane	mild
date	page	wave	mile
dame	pale	Bile	mind
face	pane	bind	mine
fade	pate	bite	mire
fame	pave	cite	mite
fane	race	dice	nice
gale	rage	dike	nine
gate	rake	dine	pike
gave	rate	dire	pile
hale	raze	dive	pine
hate	rave	file	pint
lade	sage	find	pipe
lake	sake	fine	rice
lame	sale	fire	Bold
lane	same	five	bolt
late	sane	hide	bone

code	gold	lore	port
cold	gore	mode	robe
colt	hold	mole	roll
cone	hole	mope	tone
cope	hose	more	Cube
cove	home	most	cure
core	hone	mote	duke
dome	host	nose	dupe
dote	hove	poll	fume
doze	joke	pope	fuse
fold	jolt	pore	lute
fort	lone	pork	lure

One and two make three.
Six and four make ten.
Four and five make nine.
Do you ask if you are to die?
Yes, you and I, and all men must die.
If I see a boy do ill I will try not to do so.
Must I not do as I am bid?
When you are bid to do well.
But you must do no ill.
I will try to make the best use of time.
Play not with bad boys.
I will be sure to tell no lies.
Do not hurt poor puss.
A rat is in the trap.
Puss will kill it.
I thank you for this book.
I will try to read it well.
You have read quite well.

CHAPTER III.

Easy Words of Two Syllables,

Accent on the first syllable.

Al um	gos lin	nap kin	dit ty
an vil	gos pel	nos tril	diz zy
bil let	gos sip	nov el	dus ky
bod kin	hab it	nut meg	en try
buf fet	ham let	op tic	ed dy
cab in	in dex	on set	en vy
cam el	ken nel	pan el	fan cy
can cel	kid nap	pan ic	fer ry
can did	lan cet	par ish	fol ly
can not	lap pet	pen man	gip sy
civ il	lav ish	rad ish	han dy
col ic	lev el	ras cal	hap py
com et	lim it	reb el	hur ry
com ic	lim pid	rev el	jel ly
con sul	lin en	rob in	jet ty
dam ask	lin net	sat in	jol ly
dam sel	lin tel	sig nal	lev y
den tal	liv id	sol id	lil y
des pot	med al	son net	lob by
dis mal	men tal	tal ent	mer ry
em met	mer it	val id	pan try
ep ic	mil let	Al ley	par ry
ex it	mit ten	an gry	pet ty
fil let	mod el	ber ry	pig my
fin ish	mod est	can dy	pit y
fis cal	mor al	car ry	sil ly
fun nel	mus ket	cur ry	six ty
gar ret	mus lin	dal ly	sor ry

sul ky	va ry	en ter	du el
sul try	Bri er	ev er	du cal
sur ly	fe ver	gan der	fa tal
tab by	gro cer	gen der	fi nal
tal ly	jo ker	gin ger	fo cus
tar ry	li on	hin der	fu el
tip sy	ma jor	hop per	gru el
ug ly	mi nor	lad der	le gal
Bo ny	old er	lat ter	li bel
cro ny	o ver	lep er	na sal
du ly	own er	let ter	pa gan
du ty	pa per	liv er	po et
fu ry	pi per	nev er	re al
glo ry	po lar	of fer	ro ses
ho ly	por ter	ot ter	ru in
i vy	so ber	pep per	ru ral
ju ry	ta per	pot ter	to tal
la dy	to per	riv er	tri al
la zy	wa fer	sil ver	ve nal
na vy	Ad der	sis ter	vi al
no bly	am ber	Be ing	vi tal
po ny	ban ner	bi as	u nit
po sy	bat ter	co gent	ex ile
ro sy	bet ter	cru el	mot to
sto ry	bit ter	de cent	tad pol
ti dy	but ter	di al	um pire

Accent on the second syllable.

Ab surd	af fix	as sess	at tack
ac cept	al lot	as sist	at tent
ac cess	ar rest	at tend	a wake
ad mit	as sent	at test	be fit

con cur	in dent	de base	pro cure
con fess	in sert	de bate	pro duce
con sent	in sist	de cide	pro pose
con tend	in tend	de cry	pro vide
con tent	it self	de face	pro voke
cor rect	in vent	de file	re cite
dis band	oc cur	de lay	re deem
dis miss	sub mit	de pose	re duce
dis til	suc cess	de sire	re fine
ex act	un bid	de pute	re gale
ex cel	un fit	de ride	re late
ex cess	un less	de vise	re mind
ex pect	un til	de vote	re mote
ex pel	Be have	e late	re pose
ex tend	be fore	e lude	re tire
for get	be hold	mo rose	re vile
in cur	be hind	pre side	sa lute

A bird can both walk and fly.
Boys must not hurt the birds.
Some bad boys rob them of their eggs.
I saw a boy shut up a bird in a cage.
Do birds like to be shut up?
No, they like to fly about.
We must do as we like to be done to.
Be kind to all men.
Did you see the boys ride in the cart?
I will give you my top for your ball.
I do not like to hear one fret.
I do not like to be here.
Let us go to bed, and take our rest.
Take care of your book, and keep it clean.

CHAPTER IV.

Easy Words of Three Syllables.

Accent on the first syllable.

Ac tu al	fel o ny	par i ty
ag o ny	her e sy	pen u ry
am i ty	her e tic	pol i cy
an i mal	his to ry	rar i fy*
an nu al	id i ot	rar i ty
bat te ry	im i tate	rat i fy*
big ot ry	in di go	sal a ry
bod i ly	in fa my	sat is fy*
bot a ny	in fi del	sim i le
cal i co	in ju ry	ter ri fy*
can o py	leg a cy	van i ty
cas u al	len i ty	vil i fy*
cav i ty	lev i ty	Ab di cate
cen tu ry	lib er al	ac ci dent
cit a del	lib er ty	ac cu rate
col o ny	lin e al	ad mi ral
com e dy	lit a ny	ad vo cate
dep u ty	lit er al	an ces tor
eb o ny	lot te ry	ap pe tite
ed i fy*	lux u ry	ben e fit
ed it or	mel o dy	but ter fly*
el e gy	mem o ry	cal en dar
en e my	min u et	cal o mel
en mi ty	mon o dy	cal um ny
en er gy	mor ti fy*	can is ter
ev e ry	nur se ry	cat a ract
fal la cy	or i gin	cen tu ry
fam i ly	par o dy	cer ti fy*

* *y* like *i* long.

char i ot
char i ty
chas ti ty
cin na mon
com i cal
com pe tent
con fi dent
con ju gal
con so nant
con tra ry
con ver sant
cur ren cy
daf fo dil
det ri ment
dif fi dent
dis so lute
dis so nant
em er ald
em pe ror
es cu lent
ex cel lent
fab ri cate
flat te ry
gal le ry
gen tle man
glob u lar
grad u ate
im mi nent
im pu dent
in ci dent
in dus try

in fan cy
in no cent
in ter val
lat i tude
lav en der
lex i con
lig a ment
man ful ly
man i fest
med i cal
men di cant
mil i tant
mil li ner
min is ter
mis cre ant
mod er ate
mod est ly
mon u ment
mus cu lar
nov el ty
ob du rate
ob li gate
ob so lete
op po site
par a dox
pen du lum
pov er ty
rid i cule
sen si ble
sig na ture
stim u late

tam a rind
ter mi nate
ul ti mate
ven er ate
vic to ry
vin di cate
A pri cot
ca pa ble
cru ci ble
cru ci fy*
cru el ty
cu po la
de cen cy
de vi ate
du pli cate
du ra ble
fru gal ly
fu mi gate
fu ner al
ju ni per
la zi ness
le gal ly
li bra ry
li on ess
lo cal ly
me di ate
mu ta ble
mu ti late
no bod y
nu mer al
o di um

* *y* like *i* long.

o pi ate	pu tre fy*	u ni son
o pi um	ra di ant	va can cy
o ver plus	ru di ment	va ri ance
pe ri od	ru mi nate	va ri ant
pli a ble	se cre sy	ve ni al
pli an cy	stu pi fy*	vi o lence
pri ma ry	the o ry	vi o lent

Accent on the second syllable.

A ban don	e lev en	bra va do
a bol ish	e lix ir	cre a tor
ac cus tom	e met ic	de co rum
ad mon ish	e nig ma	de ni al
an gel ic	ex act ly	i de al
ap pen dix	ex ot ic	il le gal
as sem bly	in trin sic	in de cent
a sun der	mag net ic	in hu man
bo tan ic	re mem ber	po ta to
co hab it	re sem ble	se du cer
cos met ic	to bac co	tes ta tor
de can ter	a bu sive	tor na do
do mes tic	ad he rent	tri bu nal
e las tic	ap pa rent	un ti dy

Ann, will you sing me a song?
Will you make me a pen of this quill?
A fox will catch hens and geese.
Here is a fine ripe plum.
Jane has made a nice plum tart.
Do not blot your new book.
How sweet the birds sing.
Lay up the book, it is time to dine.

* *y* like *i* long.

3

CHAPTER V.
Vowel a.

a long.

Ache	flame	flake	space
bake	frame	rare	snare
bare	glade	range	spade
blade	glare	scape	spake
blame	grace	scare	spare
brace	grade	scarce	stage
brave	grape	scate	stake
care	grave	shade	stale
change	hare	shake	stare
chaste	mare	shame	state
crane	pare	share	stave
crape	phrase	shave	strange
crate	place	slake	trace
crave	plane	slate	trade
dare	plate	slave	vague
fare	prate	snake	ware

a short.

Ant	hasp	shag	trap
adze	have	slam	vast
back	lash	slab	vamp
bade	lass	slap	waft
bask	last	snap	Badge
bran	mask	span	batch
damp	mast	spat	black
fast	pant	stag	bland
flam	raft	swam	blank
flax	rank	tack	blast
gnat	rasp	task	brack

branch	craft	grass	spasm
brand	crank	hatch	sprang
brass	dance	match	sprat
catch	drank	plank	stack
chaff	flank	plant	staff
champ	flask	scalp	stand
chance	flash	scant	strand
chant	frank	scrag	thank
chasm	glance	scrap	track
clang	gland	shaft	tract
clank	glass	shall	trash
clash	gnash	shank	twang
clasp	grand	slack	wrack
class	grant	slang	wrath
crack	grasp	smack	wrap

Ann, play with the babe.
Take him in your lap.
Do not hurt him.
Catch the cat for him.
Dress your doll.
What is its name?
Help me dress me.
Here is a sharp axe.
Do not cut you.
See the lambs play.
Ride on the horse.
See that frog hop.
I trod on a snake.
Make me a sled.
Pick some plums.
Tell no lies.

Shake the tree.
Crack this nut.
The gnats bite.
Turn the crank.
Ring the bell.
Bake me a cake.
Buy me a top.
All the boys are here.
Let us play ball.
Choose sides.
See the ball hop.
I am tired.
Let us go home.
I am not well.
Put up your book.
Use no ill words.

a middle.

Arc	dark	lark	calve
are	darn	mar	carve
ark	dart	mark	charge
arm	far	mart	charm
art	farm	par	chart
balm	gape	park	halve
bar	garb	part	large
bark	ha	scar	march
barn	hard	spar	marle
calf	hark	star	psalm
calm	harm	tar	salve
car	harp	tart	shark
card	hart	yard	sharp
cart	jar	yarn	smart
carp	lard	Barge	spark

a broad.

All	hall	talk	warn
ball	halt	wall	warp
bald	malt	walk	wart
call	pall	war	wharf
chalk	salt	ward	dwarf
fall	stall	warm	thwart

The Lord will love them that fear him.
He minds all we say and do.
We must love all men, if they do not love us,
And we must pray for them that hate us.
We must make the best use of our time.
Do not read too fast, nor with a tone.
Read slow, and speak plain.

CHAPTER VI.

Vowel e.

e long.

Cede	reve	scheme	sphere
cere	scene	sere	theme
glebe	mere	she	these

e short.

Elf	slept	fledge	herd
else	tend	hedge	herse
jet	tent	hence	jerk
bred	test	ledge	nerve
cell	vend	pence	perch
cent	vent	pledge	pert
crest	vest	sedge	serge
debt	weld	shelf	serve
dress	well	shred	sherd
edge	went	sketch	smerk
elm	wept	smell	sperm
flesh	wrest	spend	stern
fresh	wren	swell	swerve
helm	Belch	swept	term
kept	blend	tempt	terse
knell	check	tenth	verb
left	chess	twelve	verse
mesh	chest	wedge	verge
mess	crept	whelm	were
prest	dense	err	wert
press	dregs	erst	yelk
reck	dwell	fern	yell
reft	fence	germ	yelp
rend	fetch	herb	yest

3*

CHAPTER VII.

Vowel i.

i long.

Blight	light	tight	wire
blind	might	tribe	wise
bride	nigh	trice	Blithe
bright	pride	twice	ninth
brine	prime	twine	scribe
child	right	vice	shrine
climb	rise	vile	slice
drive	side	vine	stride
flight	sigh	while	strike
fight	shine	white	strife
fright	slice	wide	whilst
grind	slide	wild	write
high	smile	wife	prize
kind	snipe	wine	price
knife	spright	wipe	night

i short.

Blink	hinge	stick	wrist
brink	kiln	strip	Bridge
brisk	knit	swim	clinch
chink	print	tinge	cringe
cling	prism	trill	fifth
crick	rinse	twig	flinch
crisp	skiff	wick	fringe
drill	skill	wince	sixth
drink	sling	wink	spring
fling	split	wish	string
flint	sprig	witch	swing
film	stiff	writ	whist

CHAPTER VIII.
Vowel o.

o long.

Borne	grove	sloth	torn
both	ghost	slope	trope
broke	home	smoke	vote
choke	knoll	smote	wore
chose	know	snore	worn
close	known	sold	wove
clove	note	sore	yoke
comb	probe	spoke	Brogue
droll	prone	sport	rogue
drone	prose	stole	stroll
drove	scold	store	sworn
fold	scope	stove	sword
folks	score	stow	throve
force	scroll	told	thrown
globe	shore	tole	vogue
grope	shorn	tore	wrote

o short.

Block	knock	shock	dodge
cost	knot	stock	hodge
cross	moss	song	lodge
dock	notch	solve	prompt
dross	odd	tongs	sconce
flock	prong	throb	shone
frock	romp	Blotch	throng
gloss	scoff	copse	wrong

o middle.

Do	prove	whom
lose	who	womb
move	whose	tomb

CHAPTER IX.

Vowel u.

u long.

Flute	june	puke	tube
huge	plume	pure	tune

u short.

Blunt	hurt	smut	clutch
blush	husk	snuff	crutch
brunt	hush	snug	drudge
brush	jump	spun	drunk
burgh	junk	spur	dunce
burst	lump	spurn	grudge
churn	lurch	stud	mumps
crumb	numb	stuff	plunge
crush	nurse	strut	punch
crust	plumb	stun	purge
curse	pulse	such	shrug
curve	pump	sunk	shrunk
drum	purse	sung	sprung
durst	rush	truck	spunge
dusk	scull	trunk	struck
flush	scum	truss	stung
flux	scrub	Bulge	surge
hulk	shun	bunch	swung
hung	shut	church	trudge
hunt	slut	clump	wrung

u middle.

Bull	full	push	put
bush	pull	puss	

CHAPTER X.

Irregular Sounds of the Vowels.

a like *o* short.

Swan	wan	was	wast
swap	wand	wash	watch
wad	want	wasp	what

i like *e* short.

Birth	gird	girt	skirt
firm	girl	mirth	whirl

e, i, and *o,* like *u* short.

Clerk	sir	love	ton
her	spirt	monk	tongue
hers	stir	month	won
Bird	Bomb	none	wont
birch	come	one	word
dirge	done	once	work
dirk	dost	rhomb	world
dirt	doth	shove	worm
first	dove	some	worse
flirt	front	son	wort
shirt	glove	sponge	worth

o like *a* broad.

Born	fork	lord	short
chord	for	morn	snort
cord	form	nor	sort
cork	horn	scorch	storm
corn	horse	scorn	torch

u like *o* middle.

Brute	prude	rude	spruce
crude	prune	rule	truce

CHAPTER XI.

Proper Diphthongs.

oi and *oy.*

Boil	join	oint	Boy
broil	joint	point	cloy
choice	joist	poise	coy
coil	loin	soil	joy
coin	moil	spoil	toy
foil	moist	toil	troy
groin	noise	voice	
hoist	oil	void	

ou and *ow.*

Bound	louse	scout	clown
cloud	mount	shout	cow
count	mouse	snout	crowd
crouch	mouth	sound	crown
flour	noun	sour	down
foul	ounce	south	fowl
found	out	spout	frown
fount	plough	stout	gown
gout	pound	THOU	now
ground	proud	trout	owl
hound	round	wound	scowl
house	rout	Brow	town
loud	scour	brown	vow

Here is a bee on this fine rose.
Can you tell me how old I am?
When this day is past it will come no more.

The sun shines. It is time to get up. Jane, come and dress Charles. Wash his face and hands. Comb his hair. Tie his frock. Now Charles, we will go down stairs. Fetch that chair. Sit down. Here is some bread and milk. Do not spill the milk. Hold the spoon in your right hand. The crust is hard : but the milk will soak it. Do not throw the bread on the floor. We should eat bread, and not waste it.

There is a poor fly in the milk. Take it out. Put it on this dry cloth. Poor thing! it is not quite dead. It moves; it shakes its wings; it wants to dry them; see how it wipes them with its feet. Put it on the floor where the sun shines. Then it will be dry and warm. Poor fly! I am glad it was not dead. I hope it will soon be well.

Where is puss? There she is. Do not pull her by the tail; that will hurt her. Charles does not like to be hurt; and puss does not like to be hurt. I saw a boy hurt a poor cat: he took hold of her tail; so she put out her sharp claws, and made his hand bleed. Give puss some milk. She likes milk. Now that Charles is so kind to her, she will not scratch him, nor bite him. She purrs and looks glad.

CHAPTER XII.
Improper Diphthongs and Triphthongs.

ai, au, ay, ea, ei, ey, ua, and *uai,* like long *a.*

Aid	main	Bay	tear
aim	maize	bray	wear
air	nail	clay	deign
bail	paid	day	eight
bait	pail	dray	feign
baize	pain	gay	feint
braid	pair	hay	heir
brain	paint	lay	neigh
chain	plain	may	rein
claim	plait	nay	skein
chair	rail	pay	THeir
drain	rain	pray	veil
fail	raise	play	vein
fair	sail	ray	weigh
faint	saint	say	weight
faith	slain	slay	Grey
flail	stain	spray	hey
frail	stair	stay	prey
gain	tail	sway	sley
gait	train	way	THEy
grain	trait	Bear	trey
hail	vain	break	whey
hair	wail	great	quake
lair	waist	pear	square
maid	wait	steak	quaint
mail	gauge	swear	quail

au, aw, oa, ou, and *ua,* like broad *a.*

Caught	sauce	drawn	Broad
cause	vaunt	fawn	groat
clause	Awe	flaw	Bought
daub	awl	gnaw	brought
fault	bawd	hawk	fought
fraud	bawl	jaw	nought
gauze	brawl	law	ought
laud	claw	lawn	sought
haul	crawl	pawn	thought
maul	dawn	raw	wrought
pause	draw	straw	quart

au, ea, and *ua,* like middle *a.*

Aunt	gaunt	jaunt	Heart
daunt	haunch	laugh	hearth
flaunt	haunt	launch	guard

ea, ee, ei, ey, ie, uea, and *uee,* like long *e.*

Beach	deal	hear	mean
bead	dear	heat	meat
beak	each	knead	neat
bean	ear	lead	pea
beard	east	leaf	peace
beast	eat	leak	peach
beat	fear	lean	peak
bleat	feast	least	peal
cease	feat	lease	plea
cheap	flea	leap	plead
cheat	glean	leave	reach
clear	heal	mead	read
deaf	heap	meal	ream

4

reap	deed	seen	key
rear	deem	screen	Bier
seal	deep	sheep	brief
seat	deer	sheet	chief
shear	eek	sheer	fief
sheath	eel	sleek	field
spear	feed	sleep	fiend
steal	feel	sleet	fierce
tea	flee	sleeve	frieze
teach	fleece	speech	grief
tear	fleet	speed	grieve
tease	free	spleen	lief
treat	freeze	sneer	liege
weal	glee	steed	lieve
weak	green	steel	mien
wean	greet	steer	niece
wheat	heed	street	pier
yea	heel	sneeze	pierce
year	jeer	sweep	piece
Beach	keep	sweet	priest
beef	*k*nee	teens	siege
beer	*k*neel	teeth	shield
beet	leek	tree	shriek
bleed	meek	veer	tier
breed	meet	weed	thief
breeze	need	week	wield
cheek	peel	weep	yield
cheer	peer	wheel	Queen
cheese	reed	Ceil	queer
creed	seek	seine	squeal
creep	seem	seize	squeak

_ea, ai, ay, ie, eo,_ and _ue,_ like short _e._

Bread	earn	search	said
breast	head	stead	says
death	heard	sweat	friend
dread	health	tread	tierce
earth	learn	threat	feoff
earl	pearl	yearn	guess

ie, eye, ui, uy, and _ei,_ like long _i._

Die	pie	buy	quire
fie	tie	guide	quite
hie	vie	guile	height
lie	eye	guise	sleight

_ee, ie,_ and _ui,_ like short _i._

Been	build	guild	quick
sieve	built	guilt	quill

_oa, oe, oo, ou, ow, ew, uo,_ and _eau,_ like long _o._

Boat	goal	roach	roe
boar	goat	road	sloe
board	hoar	roam	toe
boast	hoard	roan	throe
bloat	hoarse	roar	Door
broach	lead	roast	floor
cloak	loaf	shoat	course
coach	loam	soak	court
coal	loath	soap	dough
coarse	moan	soar	four
coast	moat	toast	fourth
croak	oak	woad	gourd
foal	oar	Doe	mould
foam	oath	foe	mourn
goad	poach	hoe	poult

source	grow	show	throw
soul	grown	slow	sew
тнoug_h_	growth	snow	shew
Bowl	_k_now	sow	strew
blow	low	sown	quote
crow	owe	stow	quoth
flow	own	strow	beau
glow	row	tow	

ou and *ua* like short *ò*.

Cough	trough	squash	squat

oo, *ou*, *oe*, *eu*, *ew*, *ue*, and *ui*, like middle *ọ*.

Bloom	gloom	pool	stool.
book	groom	poor	swoon
boom	groove	proof	took
boon	hook	rood	tool
boor	hoop	roof	tooth
boot	hoot	rook	troop
brood	loo	root	woof
brook	look	scнool	croup
choose	loom	shook	group
cook	loon	shoot	soup
cool	loop	sloop	tour
coop	loose	smooтн	throu_gh_
coot	mood	soon	you
crook	moon	scot	your
doom	moor	sooтн	youth
droop	moose	spool	shoe
food	noon	spoon	_r_heum
fool	noose	stoop	brew

chew	shrew	rue	cruise
crew	shrewd	true	fruit
screw	yew	bruise	

eu, ew, ue, ui, ewe, ieu, and *iew,* like long *u.*

Deuce	grew	stew	hue
feud	knew	lewd	sue
blew	hew	blue	juice
clew	mew	cue	sluice
dew	pew	due	ewe
flew	slew	flue	lieu
few	spew	glue	view

oe, oo, and *ou,* like short *u.*

Does	flood	scourge	touch
blood	rough	tough	young

oo, and *ou,* like middle *u.*

Foot	stood	could
good	wood	would
hood	wool	should

READING LESSONS.

Come to me, Charles. Come and read.
Here is a new book. Take care not to tear
it. Good boys do not spoil their books.
Speak plain. Take pains and try to read
well. Stand still. Do not read so fast.
Mind the stops. Charles has read a page
now. This is a page. This is a leaf. A
page is one side of a leaf. Shut the book.
Put it up. By and by you may read more.

4*

Shall we walk ? No ; not now. I think it
will rain soon. See how black the sky is.
Now it rains. How fast it rains. Rain comes
from the clouds. The ducks love rain. Ducks
swim, and geese swim. Can Charles swim ?
No, Charles is not a duck, nor a goose ; so he
must take care not to go too near the pond,
lest he should fall in. I do not know that we
could get him out ; if we could not he would
die. When Charles is as big as James, he
shall learn to swim.

It does not rain now. The sky is blue.
Let us take a walk in the fields ; and see the
sheep, and the lambs, the cows, and trees,
and birds. Call Tray. He shall go with
us. He wags his tail. He is glad to see us,
and to go with us. Tray likes those who
feed him and are kind to him. Do not walk
on the grass now. It is too high, and quite
wet. Walk in this dry path. There is a
worm. Do not tread on it. Can Charle
climb that wall? O what a large field. Thi
is not grass. No ; it is corn. It will be ripe
soon. Bread is made of corn. I dare sa
Charles does not know how bread is made
Well, some time I will tell him. Shall w

the bees sting us ? No, they will not, if w
do not hurt them. Wasps will not sting us
if we do not hurt them. There is a was

on my arm. Now it is gone. It has not stung me. Now let us go home.

The clock strikes. It is time to dine. Is the cloth laid? Where are the knives, and forks, and plates. Call Ann. Are your hands clean? Sit down. The soup is hot; wait till it is cool. Will you have some lamb, and some pease? Do not make a noise with your lips when you eat. Take some bread. Break it, do not bite it. Jane must shake the cloth out of doors. The fowls will pick up the crumbs. Now let us go and play with George.

There is a poor blind man at the door. He is quite blind. He does not see the sky, nor the ground, nor the trees, nor men. He does not see us though we are so near to him. A boy leads him from door to door. O, it is a sad thing to be blind. We will give the blind man some bread and cheese. Now he is gone. He is a great way off. Poor blind man? Come in, Charles. Shut the door. I wish the poor blind man had a warm house to live in, and kind friends to take care of him, and teach him to work. Then he would not beg from door to door.

When you are told of a fault, you must take pains to mend it.

The tree is known by its fruit.

CHAPTER XIII.

Dissyllables accented on the First Syllable.

Both syllables short.

Ab ject	clem ent	fer ret	hon est
ab scess	clos et	fer vent	hunts man
ab sence	cob web	flan nel	hus band
ac cent	cof fin	flip pant	in cense
ad vent	com bat	for eign	in sect
an nals	com ment	for est	in stant
an vil	com plex	fos sil	in step
bal ance	con duct	fran tic	in sult
bal last	con test	friend ship	judg ment
ban ish	con vent	fur nish	ker nel
bar rack	con vex	gam ut	kin dred
bar ren	cred it	gant let	kitch en
bed stead	crick et	gib bet	learn ing
bon net	cun ning	gim let*	log ic
break fast	cur rant	gran dam	mag ic
breath less	cur rent	grav el	mag net
brick bat	cut lass	gul let	mal ice
can vass	diph thong	gus set	mas tiff
cap stan	dis tant	har ass	max im
car at	dock et	hap less	mer chant
cask et	dul cet	hec tic	mim ic
cav il	dul ness	hedg es	ob ject
chap el	em blem	hel met	ob long
chap let	er rand	help less	of fice
cher ub	ex tant	herds man	pack et
chis el	fab ric	her mit	per fect
clar et	fam ine	her ring	pil grim
clas sic	fam ish	hick up	plac id

*g hard.

plan et	run net	skit tish	ten et
rab bit	sab bath	sud den	trip*h* thong
rack et	sal ad	sul tan	vas sal
rap in*e*	san dal	sul len	vel lum
rem nant	scan dal	tac it	wel kin
rig id	sen tence	tan gent	wick ed
ring let	shil ling	tar iff	wit ness

Both syllables long.

A gu*e*	f*ea* ture	mo hair	se*iz* ure
a zure	fi nite	na ture	so lo
cli mate	fore si*gh*t	ne gro	te nure
clo *s*ure	fo*ur* score	por trait	tri une
co co*a*	four teen	pri mate	twi li*gh*t
cre*a* ture	fu ture	*p*seu do	ty ro
cu rate	le*i s*ure	ra *s*ure	va cate
fe male	li brate	sa go	vi brate

The first syllable long, y in the second like e long.

B*eau* ty	gree dy	low ly	r*ai*n y
clear ly	gre*a s*y	me*a*l y	safe ly
dear ly	hi*gh* ly	mi*gh* ty	slow ly
dai ly	home ly	most ly	smo ky
dain ty	kind ly	ne*a*t ly	spi cy
dai ry	late ly	need y	s*w*eet ly
dai *s*y	le*a*k y	new ly	tro phy
fee bly	like ly	pas try	tu*es* d*a*y
fri d*a*y	live ly	pure ly	we*a* ry

The first short, y in the second like e long.

Bel fry	cler gy	ear ly	fan cy
cher ry	cop y	ed dy	fil thy
cit y	drop sy	em*p* ty	fur ry

gen try	hur ry	qûick ly	stud y
glos sy	mer cy	ral ly	sul ky
guil ty	pop py	read y	thurs day
heav y	prox y	rud dy	ves try
hun gry	pup py	scur vy	wednes day

The first long, the second like *u* short.

Blithe some	hol ster	old er	stran ger
bol ster	hu mour	pa tron	tai lor
cham ber	la bour	pray er	teach er
ce dar	lu cre	qûa ker	tire some
ci der	man ger	qûa ver	thriv er
ci pher	ma tron	read er	tra der
coul ter	may or	reap er	trai tor
ea ger*	mea gre	ru mour	ti ger*
dan ger	me tre	sa vour	tu mour
dra per	mi ser	sci on	tu tor
fa vour	ni tre	scra per	vi per
fla vour	oa kum	se rous	vi nous
grind er	o chre	smo ker	wa fer

The first short, the second like *u* short.

Af ter	bot tom	clam our	em bers
am ber	buck ler	cob bler	er rour
an chor	buck ram	cus tom	fac tor
an ger*	bux om	dag ger*	fath om
an swer	can non	debt or	fer vour
bab bler	cen ser	din ner	fin ger*
beg gar	chap ter	doc tor	flag on
blis ter	chat ter	drag on	flat ter
blun der	chest nut	earl dom	flut ter
blus ter	clap per	el der	fur ther

*g hard.

gam mon	mem ber	ran som	sun der
ham mer	meth od	ren der	sup per
hav ock	mon ster	rec tor	tem per
heif er	mor tar	rob ber	ten don
hon our	mur der	scat ter	ten our
huck ster	nec tar	schol ar	trench er
hunt er	num ber	scol lop	ter rour
jeal ous	pan ther	scis sors	twit ter
king dom	par rot	sec ond	um ber
lad der	plas ter	sec tor	ven om
lan tern	phil ter	sel dom	vic tor
lem on	pitch er	sex ton	vig our
lim ner	plat ter	shiv er	vul gar
lim ber	pon der	skim mer	wis dom
lob ster	pop lar	slan der	wrest ler
lum ber	prop er	slip per	zeal ot
man ner	puck er	snuf fers	zeal ous
mat ter	quiv er	splen dour	
mel on	ran cour	spig ot	

The first long, the second short.

A gent	dur ance	hear ing	light ning
an gel	feel ing	host ess	lu pine
bail iff	fla grant	hoarse ness	mean ing
blind ness	flu ent	huge ness	mo dish
blue ness	flu id	hu man	mo ment
bright ness	fru gal	i tem	mu sic
bri dal	glean ing	keen ness	name less
cam bric	gi ant	kind ness	no tice
ceil ing	gra tis	la tent	pa pist
creep ing	heal ing	li lach	pa rent

peel ing	ri ses	stu pid	va grant
peev ish	sa cred	thiev ish	writ ing
pierc ing	sci ence	ti dings	yeo man
plain ness	se cret	tri dent	ze nith
pli ant	shape less	tu mult	stu dent
pre cept	si lent	tu nic	qui et
pu pil	spe cies	va cant	na tive

The first short, the second long.

Bar row	dic tate	mot to	tal low
bel low	el bow	mun dane	tell tale
birth right	em pire	non suit	tinc ture
birth place	frus trate	pic ture	tis sue
brim stone	gan grene	pil low	turn pike
bug bear	guin ea	pleas ure	ut most
cof fee	hol low	pur blind	ven ture
chil blain	im post	sor row	ves ture
con clave	junc ture	spar row	vol ume
con trite	man date	stat ue	vul ture
cup board	meas ure	stat ure	wel fare
cur tail	mid wife	stat ute	win now
del uge	mix ture	stric ture	yel low

The first middle, the second short.

Arch ing	dark ness	look ing	psal mist
art less	dar ling	mar gin	pud ding
bloom ing	far THing	mar quis	sar casm
bul let	fool ish	mar shal	scar let
bush el	gar land	mar vel	spark ling
card ing	gar ment	par cel	tar get
car tridge	harm less	pars nip	tar nish
charm ing	jaun dice	par tridge	var nish

The first midd'e, the second like *u* short.

Ar bour	bo som	faTH er	lar ger
ar dour	butch er	far THer	mar tyr
ar mour	carp er	gar ter	mas ter
bar ber	charg er	har bour	par lour
bar ter	farm er	har lot	part ner

The first broad, the second like *u* short.

Al tar	au tumn	hal ter	war bler
al der	daugh ter	law yer	ward er
au ger*	draw er	pau per	wa ter
au thor	fal ter	sau cer	warm er

The first broad, the second short.

Au dit	plau dit	walk ing	warm ness
call ing	salt ish	wal nut	warn ing
fault less	talk ing	warm ing	yawn ing

a in the first like *o* short, the second short.

Wad ding	want ing	war ren	wasp ish
wal let	war rant	wash ing	watch ing

Love your parents. They love you, and have taken care of you ever since you were born. They loved you and took care of you when you were little helpless infants, that could not talk, nor walk about, nor do any thing but cry, and give a great deal of trouble.

Obey your parents. They know better what is proper for you than you do; and they wish you to be good, and wise, and happy.

* g hard.

THE SUN.

The sun rises in the east, and when he rises it is day. He shines upon the trees, and
the houses, and upon the water; and every
thing looks sparkling and beautiful when he
shines upon it. He gives us light and heat;
it is he that makes it warm. He makes the
fruit and the corn ripen. If he did not shine
upon the fields and gardens, nothing would
grow.

Sometimes he takes off his crown of bright
rays, and wraps up his head in thin silver
clouds, and then we may look at him : but
when there are no clouds, and he shines
with all his brightness at noon day, we cannot look at him, for he would dazzle our eyes,
and make us blind. Only the eagle can look
at him then : the eagle with his strong piercing eye can look at him always.

When the sun is going to rise in the morning, and make it day, the lark flies up in the
sky to meet him, and sings sweetly in the air;
and the cock crows loud to tell every body
that he is coming. But the owl and the bat
fly away when they see him, and hide themselves in old walls and hollow trees ; and the
lion and the tiger go into their dens and
caves, where they sleep all day.

He shines in all countries, all over the
earth. He is the most beautiful and glorious
creature that can be seen in the whole
world.

CHAPTER XIV.

Dissyllables accented on the second syllable.

Both syllables short.

Ab rupt	a g*h*ast	ex press	ob struct
ab scond	al lege	ex tinct	oc cur
ab *s*olve	as cend	for give*	of fen*c*e
a byss	at tack	har ang*ue*	po*s* sess
ac qûit	at tem*p*t	him self	suc oinct
ad dress	cor rupt	im men'se	sug gest
ad just	di*s* gust	in dulge	sus pect
ad van*c*e	dis tress	in spect	sus pend
af fect	dis pense	in struct	trans plant
af fix	dis turb	in trust	tran s*c*end
af flict	en camp	neg lect	un twist

Both syllables long.

Be g*u*ile	de grade	o blige	re cluse
be l*i*ef	de gree	pe ru*s*e	re cour*s*e
be ne*ath*	de li*gh*t	post pone	re fra*i*n
be qûe*ath*	de mi*s*e	pre pare	re l*i*ef
be *s*eech	de mure	pre scribe	re l*i*eve
be s*i*ege	de range	pre *s*ume	re ma*i*n
be stow	de sign	pro cla*i*m	re proach
be tween	e squîre	pro fane	re pr*i*eve
be wa*i*l	fore go	pro fuse	re quire
de ce*a*se	fore *k*now	pro mote	re *s*ign
de ceit	fore see	pro rog*ue*	re stra*i*n
de ce*i*ve	ma*i*n ta*i*n	re ce*i*pt	re tr*i*eve
de cla*i*m	mo rose	re ce*i*ve	se cure
de er*ea*se	o paq*ue*	re cla*i*m	se date

*g hard.

The first short, the second long.

A base	a side	con geal	im pute
a bate	as sign	con sign	im pure
a bide	as sume	con sole	in clude
a chieve	as suage	con strain	in flict
ab jure	at tain	con sume	in û·re q i
ab stain	at tire	con trive	mis name
ab struse	a wake	con trol	mis take
ac cuse	blas pheme	con vene	mis use
ac quaint	cam paign	dif fuse	ob lique
ac quire	cal cine	dis close	ob scene
ad here	cham paign	dis creet	ob scure
a dore	cash ier	dis grace	ob tain
ad vice	com mune	dis guise	op pose
ad vise	com plaint	dis place	per ceive
af fright	com pile	dis please	per suade
a fraid	com plete	dis suade	per tain
ag grieve	com ply	do main	pur sue
a like	com port	en close	sub lime
a live	com pose	en dure	sub scribe
al lies	com prise	en force	sus tain
al lude	com pute	en rage	trus tee
al lure	con ceit	en tice	up braid
a lone	con ceive	en throne	un chaste
a maze	con cise	en treat	un close
a muse	con clude	ex claim	un known
ap pease	con fide	ex cite	un safe
a rise	con fine	ex treme	un tie
a rose	con fute	im peach	un twine
ar range	con dign	im pose	un yoke

The first long, the second short.

Be head	de scend	pre tence	re press
be gin	de tect	pre vent	re print
be quest	de test	pro ject	re pulse
be set	e clipse	pro tect	re quest
be witch	e ject	pro test	re sist
be yond	e quip	re bel	re solve
de camp	e rect	re cur	re turn
de duct	fore tel	re fer	tre pan
de fend	gro tesque	re fresh	u surp
de fence	pre dict	re fund	re lent
de ject	pre fer	re gret	re miss
de pend	pre judge	re ject	re mit
de press	pre serve	re lax	re pel

The first short, the second middle.

A larm	em bark	a loof	im prove
a far	en large	ap prove	mon soon
a part	guit ar	bab oon	rack oon
ca tarrh	im part	bal loon	shal loon
com mand	mam ma	bas soon	un couth
dis arm	pa pa	buf foon	un do
dis card	un arm	dis prove	un hook
dis charge	un bar	drag oon	ca noe
em balm	a do	gal loon	a mour

The first short; in the second *a* broad, and *o* like *a* broad.

Ap pal	in thral	a broad	dis tort
ap plaud	mis cal	ab hor	in form
as sault	un taught	a dorn	per form
ex alt	with al	ex hort	sub orn
ex haust	with draw	ex tort	trans form

5*

The first long, the second broad.

| Be cause | de bauch | de fault | re cal |
| be fal | de fraud | fore warn | re ward |

The first long, the second middle.

Be calm	re gard	re tard	re move
de mand	re mark	Be hoove	re proof
de part	re mand	be fool	re prove

DUTIES OF CHILDREN.

Love your brothers and sisters. Do not tease nor vex them, nor call them names; and never let your little hands be raised to strike them. If they have any thing which you would like to have, do not be angry with

have any thing they like, share it with them.

Your parents grieve when they see you quarrel; they love you all, and wish you to love one another, and to live in peace and harmony.

Do not meddle with what does not belong to you; nor ever take other people's things without leave.

Never tell an untruth. When you are relating any thing you have seen, or heard, endeavour to tell it exactly as it was. Do not alter or invent any part, to make it, as you may think, a prettier story. If you have forgotten any part, say that you have forgotten it. Persons who love the truth, never tell a lie even in jest.

CHAPTER XV.

Accent on the first syllable.

The first short, the vowel in the second silent.

An kle	fast en	lit tle	pris on
ap ple	gen tle	list en	pur ple
bot tle	giv en*	med dle	rat tle
buc kle	glut ton	net tle	reck on
bun dle	hap pen	nim ble	sic kle
can dle	hum ble	oft en	sin gle
cot ton	ket tle	peb ble	thim ble
crum ble	kin dle	ped dle	troub le
daz zle	les son	per son	whis tle

The first long, the vowel in the second silent.

A ble	ea gle	no ble	sea son
ba con	e ven	o pen	sta ble
ba sin	e vil	peo ple	stee ple
Bi ble	fa ble	ra ven	ta ble
bro ken	fro zen	rai sin	ta ken
cho sen	i dle	rea son	to ken
cra dle	ma son	ri pen	wo ven

Compound words.—Both syllables long.

Bee hive	hail stone	rain bow
blind fold	key hole	scare crow
bride maid	leap year	sea coal
day break	life time	side board
day light	like wise	side long
eye sight	nose gay	side ways
field piece	night mare	sky light
grind stone	paste board	way lay

* g hard.

TERMINATIONAL SOUNDS.

cient and *tient*	like	*shent ;*
cial and *tial*		*shal ;*
tion, cion, cian and *sion,* . .		*shun ;*
tious, cious, ceous, and *scious,* .		*shus ;*
geon, and *gion,*		*jun ;*
tian, ...		*tchun ;*
science, and *tience,*		*shense ;*
sier and *zier,*		*zhur.*

The first syllable long.

An cient	lo tion	por tion	re gion
pa tient	mo tion	gra cious	bra sier
qûo tient	na tion	spa cious	gla zier
pa tience	no tion	spe cious	ho sier
so cial	po tion	le gion	o sier

The first syllable short.

Ac tion	op tion	unc tion	con science
cap tion	pas sion	blud geon	frac tious
dic tion	pen sion	dun geon	lus cious
fac tion	rup tion	gud geon	pre cious
fic tion	sanc tion	stur geon	vi cious
frac tion	sec tion	sur geon	chris tian
junc tion	ses sion	cap tious	fus tian
man sion	suc tion	con scious	nup tial
men tion	ten sion	fac tious	spe cial

Words in which *i* in the final syllable sounds like *y* consonant.

Bill iards	flex ion	on ion	trill ion
bill ion	flux ion	pill ion	triv ial
bil ious	fil ial	pin ion	trunn ion
clar ion	mill ion	pon iard	val iant
coll ier	min ion	scull ion	vis ion

Words in which *o* and *ou* sound like *u* short ; *ei* and *ey,* like *e* long ; *a* in the termination *age, ai, ia* and *y,* like *i* short ; and *ew* like *u* long.

Broth er	dam age	jew el	cym bal
con jure	herb age	pew ter	cyn ic
moth er	lug gage	skew er	dac tyle.
oth er	man age	bar gain	lyr ic
stom ach	rum mage	cap tain	mys tic
hon ey	til lage	car riage	phys ic
jour ney	ton nage	cer tain	sym bol
mon key	wharf age	cur tain	syn od
mon ey	ei ther	en trails	syn tax
tur key	nei ther	mar riage	syr inge
bag gage	brew er	plan tain	sys tem
cour age	few er	cyg net	cab bage

Accent on the second syllable.

o like *u* short, *i* in the second syllable like *e* long, and *ei* and *ey* like *a* long.

Af front	a bove	fas cine	ma rine
a mong	an tique	fa tigue	pur vey
a mongst	ca price	in trigue	sur vey
be come	cha grin	ma chine	in veigh

OUR DUTY TO OUR CREATOR.

Our Parents are very good to us; but God is better than our parents, and has done more for us. He gave us every thing we have. He is not a man, but he is better than any man ever was or can be.

He created the Heavens and the earth, and every thing upon the earth. He has made us more excellent than the beasts, for he has given us a soul that may know God; and

know that he is good, and wise, and great.
Our bodies will die and be laid in the grave.
But our souls are immortal ; they will never
die.   God orders every thing ; he knows every thing ; and can do every thing.   He sees
us wherever we are, by night as well as by
day ; and knows all that we say, and do and
think.

We must love God.   Good people love
him more than they do any person or thing
in the world.   They never rise in the morning, nor lie down at night, without thinking
of him, and of the good he has done for them.
Often in the day they think of him ; and love
to talk, and hear, and read of him.

We must praise God, and pray to him to
forgive us when we do wrong;   to put good
thoughts into our minds, and help us to grow
wiser and better ; to bless our parents, and
all our friends ; and give us every thing
proper for us.

We must do to all persons what God requires us to do.   The things that he requires
of us will make us good and happy.   If we
do them not, he will be displeased with us,
and punish us. He can take away our friends,
and every thing he has given us, and after
death he can make us miserable forever.
But if we try to be good, and do what he requires of us, he will help us to love him and do
his will ; he will make us happy in our minds,
and when we die he will take us to heaven.

JANE AND CHARLES READING THE BIBLE.

We must love to read the Bible. It is the
most excellent of all books. God himself
commanded good men to write it. There
we read of all the great and good things he
has done for us, and for all people. How
just, and wise, and powerful he is, and what
we must do to please him. There we read
that we are sinners, and have all broken God's
holy law. There too, we read of Christ who
came into the world to save us from our
sins. He loved us, and gave his life for us.
When we have read or heard about Christ,
and who he was, and what great things he
has done for us, we must love him, and be
thankful to him, and try to imitate him.

There is much in the Bible which you
cannot now understand; but as you grow
older, you will understand it better; and as
you grow wiser, you will love it more.

CHAPTER XVI.

Trisyllables, accented on the firs

The accented syllable short.

Ab sti nence	cham pi on	em i grate
ad a mant	cHar ac ter	em pha sis
ad jec tive	char i ot	ep i gram
af flu ence	cHem is try	ep i taph
af ter ward	chiv al ry	e qui page
ag gran dize	cler gy man	ev er green
ag i tate	cir cum flex	ex cel lence
al pha bet	cir cum spect	ex er cise
an a lyze	cir cum stance	fab u lous
an o dyne	col lo quy	fem i nine
ap a.thy	com pro mise	fir ma ment
aph o rism	con se quent	fish er man
an ar cHy	crit i cism	friv o lous
an ti type	croc o dile	fur ni ture
ar ro gant	dal li ance	gen er ous
at mo sphere	dec a logue	hand ker chie
av a rice	dem a gogue	haz ard ous
bach e lor	des ig nate	hon es ty
bash ful ness	des po tism	hur ri cane
blas phe my	diffi cult	ig no rance
blun der er	dil i gence	im ple ment
bur gla ry	dis ci pline	in di gence
cHam o mile	doc u ment	in fa mous
cat a logue	el e gance	in fi nite
cat e cHism	el e phant	in stru ment
cath o lic	el o quent	in ter view
cen tu ry	em er ald	jeal ous y

jes sa mine	par a phrase	rhet o ric
lab y rinth	par ox ysm	rid i cule
leg i ble	ped a gogue	sac cha rine
leth ar gy	ped i gree	sac ra ment
lib er tine	pen i tence	sep ul chre
lon gi tude	per quis ite	sig na ture
mack er el	pes ti lence	sol e cism
mag is trate	phleg ma tic	spec i men
mag ni tude	pleas an try	spec ta cles
man u script	por cu pine	strat a gem
mas cu line	por rin ger	sub al tern
mech an ism	prec i pice	sub se quent
mer can tile	pres ent ly	sub stan tive
mer chan dise	pris on er	sup ple ment
met a phor	prom i nent	sus te nance
mis chiev ous	promp ti tude	tan ta mount
mul ber ry	prop a gate	tech nic al
nar ra tive	prop er ty	tel e graph
na tion al	pros e lyte	tel e scope
nav i gate	pros per ous	tem pe rance
nec ta rine	prov en der	tim or ous
neg li gence	prov i dence	tran si tive
ob lo quy	pul ver ize	treach er ous
ob sti nate	pun ish ment	treach e ry
or an ges	pur ga tive	tur pen tine
or di nance	rail le ry	ul cer ous
pag ean try	rasp ber ry	ut ter ance
par a dise	ra tion al	ven om ous
par a graph	reg i ment	vict ual er
par a lyze	ret ro spect	vig il ance

6

The accented syllable long.

De i ty	u ni on	glu ti nous
de vi ate	u ni ty	gree di ness
di a dem	us u al	hu mor ous
di a per	vi o lent	i dle ness
di a ry	vo ta ry	ju ve nile
ge ni al	al ien ate†	lei sure ly
ge ni us	a que ous	lu cra tive
i ro ny	bay o net	lu di crous
i vo ry	beau te ous	lu mi nous
jo vi al	beau ti ful	mi cro scope
la i ty	care less ly	mu tin ous
le ni ent	change a ble	nu mer ous
lu na cy	co pi ous	nu tri ment
me di um	cu cum ber	nu tri tive
me ni al	cu ri ous	o di ous
me te or	dan ger ous	o dor ous
mu ti ny	de vi ous	o ver ture
mu tu al	di a mond	pa tri ot
no ta ry	di a logue	peace a ble
no ti fy §	du bi ous	po ten tate
pa pa cy	ea ger ly*	pre vi ous
pi e ty	east er ly	pu er ile
pi ra cy	eu cha rist	rheu ma tism‡
po e try	fa vour ite	rose ma ry
po pe ry	free hold er	sce ne ry
pu ri fy §	fre quen cy	teach a ble
pu ri ty	fu gi tive	the a tre
ra di us	grate ful ly	thiev ish ness
ro sa ry	glo ri ous	wea ri some

§ y like i long.   † i like y.   * g hard.   ‡ u like o middle.

The accented syllable middle.

Ar bi trate	bar ba rous	lar ce ny
ar chi tect	car bun cle	mar gin al
ar che type	car di nal	mar tyr dom
ar du ous	car pen ter	mar vel lous
ar gu ment	car ti lage	par lia ment
ar mis tice	faTH er less	par ti cle
ar mo ry	gar den er	par ti san
ar te ry	guar di an	part ner ship
ar ti choke	har le quin	phar ma cy
ar ti cle	har mo ny	laugh a ble
ar ti fice	harp si chord	mar chion ess

The first syllable like *i* short.

Cyl in der	pyr a mid	sym me try
hyp o crite	syc a more	sym pa thy
myr i ad	syc o phant	syn a gogue
mys te ry	syl la ble	typ ic al
phys ic al	syl lo gism	tyr an ny

A proper diphthong in the accented syllable.

Bois ter ous	coun ter part	joy ful ly
boun te ous	coun ter sign	lous i ness
boun ti ful	cow ard ice	moi e ty
bow er y	doubt ful ness	moun te bank
cloud i ness	dow a ger	poig nan cy
coun sel lor	drow si ness	poi son ous
coun te nance	flow er y	pow er ful
coun ter feit	house hold er	roy al ty

SELECT SENTENCES.

He that cares only for himself, has but few pleasures; and those few are of the lowest order. A good person has a tender concern for the happiness of others.

No confidence can be placed in those who are in the habit of lying.

If tales were not listened to, there would be no tale-bearers.

We may escape the censure of others, when we do wrong privately; but we cannot avoid the reproaches of our own mind.

Every desire of the heart, every secret thought, is made known to him who made us.

The most secret acts of goodness are seen and approved by the Almighty.

A kind word, nay even a kind look, often affords comfort to the afflicted.

Our best friends are those who tell us of our faults, and teach us how to correct them.

It is a great blessing to have virtuous and pious parents.

We can never treat a fellow creature ill, without offending the gracious Creator, and Father of all.

Modesty is one of the chief ornaments of youth.

Idleness is the parent of vice and misery.

The real wants of nature are soon satisfied.

Boast not of the favours you bestow.

CHAPTER XVII.
Accent on the second syllable.

The accented syllable short.

A bun dance	con fes sion	ju di cial
ac com plish	con junc tion	li cen tious*
ac *knowl* edge	con sum*p* tion	*li*eu ten ant
ad di tion	con tem plate	ma gi cian
ad mis sion	de cep tion	me chan ic
ad van tage	de clen sion	me theg lin
af fec tion	de li cious	mis car riage
am bi tion	de lin quent	mo las ses
ap pren tic*e*	dis cour age	of fi cious
as sas sin	dis cre tion	phy *si* cian
as ton ish	di*s hon* est	po*s ses* sion
as trin gent	di*s* mis sion	po*s ses* sour
at trac tion	dis tinct ly	pre dic tion
bat tal ion	dis tin guish	pre ten sion
be gin ning	em bar rass	pro gres sion
be long ing	en dea*v our*	pro phet ic
bis sex til*e*	en am *our*	pro vin cial
cha ot ic	en chant ment	pru den tial
ci vil ian	e spe cial	re duc tion
col lec tion	fla gi tious	re flec tion
com pas sion	gi gan tic*	re lig ion
com mis sion	hys ter ic	re *s*ent ment
com mit tee	in de*bt* ed	re venge ful
com pan ion	in den ture	sus pi cion
com plex ion	in dul gence	tran scend ent
com po*s* ite	in struc ter	um brel la
con di tion	in trin sic	un ple*as* ant

* *i* is in the first syllable long.

6*

The accented syllable long.

A chieve ment	de ceit ful	out ra geous
ad ja cent	de ceiv er	plan ta tion
a gree ment	de co rous	ple be ian*
ag griev ance	de mure ly	pol lu tion
al li ance	de light ful	po lite ly
a muse ment	de mean our	po ma tum
ar range ment	de po nent	pro mo tion
as sail ant	de vo tion	quo ta tion
as su rance	dis grace ful	ra pa cious
a tro cious	do na tion	re ceiv er
be hav iour	dis ci ple	re la tion
be tray er	e mo tion	re li ance
ca pa cious	en dan ger	re main der
car na tion	en fee ble	re proach ful
ca the dral	ex clu sive	sa ga cious
ces sa tion	fal la cious	sal va tion
cHi me ra	foun da tion	se rene ly
co e qual	gra da tion	se vere ly
col la tion	hu mane ly	sin cere ly
com pla cence	im pa tient	so lu tion
com plete ly	im peach ment	spec ta tor
com po nent	im pure ly	temp ta tion
con ceal ment	im pru dent	te na cious
con ceit ed	in qui ry	trans pa rent
con cre tion	le ga tion	un seem ly
con sign ment	lo qua cious	va ca tion
con tri vance	nar ra tion	vex a tious
cre a tion	ob la tion	vo ca tion
de ci pher	o blig ing	vol ca no

* *i* like *y.*

Accent on the last syllable.

The accented syllable short.

Ac qui esce	con tra dict	pic tu resque
ap pre hend	cor res pond	rec ol lect
cir cum spect	dis con tent	rec om mend
co a lesce	in di rect	rep re hend
com plai sance	in cor rect	rep re sent
com pre hend	in ter mix	un der stand
con de scend	in ter sect	vi o lin*

The accented syllable long.

Ad ver tise	dis be lief	mis be have
ap per tain	dis o blige	o ver flow
as cer tain	dis u nite	o ver hear
as sign ee	dom i neer	o ver take
auc tion eer	en gi neer	pri va teer*
brig a dier	en ter tain	ser e nade
chan de lier	gaz et teer	su per fine
co in cide	gren a dier	su per scribe
con tra vene	in ter cede	un der go
deb au chee	in tro duce	un der take
dis a gree	mas quer ade	vol un teer

SELECT SENTENCES.

To practise virtue is the way to love it.

Learning and knowledge must be attained by slow degrees ; and are the reward only of diligence and patience.

Weak minds are ruffled by trifling things.

Sincere persons are always esteemed.

They who seek wisdom will certainly find her.

* *i* in first syllable long.

The days that are past, are gone forever ; those that are to come may not come to us ; the present time only is ours : Let us therefore improve it as much as possible.

Never sport with pain and distress in any of your amusements ; nor treat even the meanest insect with wanton cruelty.

Without frugality none can be rich ; and with it very few would be poor.

How glorious an object is the sun ! but how much more glorious is that great and good Being who made it for our use.

God is the kindest and best of beings. He is our Father. He approves us when we do well ; he pities us when we err ; and he desires to make us happy forever. How greatly should we love so good and kind a Father ! and how careful should we be to please him.

They who have nothing to give can often afford relief to others by imparting what they feel.

Faithful are the wounds of a friend ; but the kisses of an enemy are deceitful. Open rebuke is better than secret love.

Seest thou a man wise in his own conceit? There is more hope of a fool than of him.

He that is slow to anger, is better than the mighty ; and he that ruleth his spirit, than he that taketh a city.

A soft answer turneth away wrath ; but grievous words stir up anger.

CHAPTER XVIII.

Words of four Syllables.

Accent on the first syllable.—The accented syllable short.

Ac cu ra cy	feb ru a ry	ob sti na cy
ad mi ra ble	fig u ra tive	or a to ry
ag ri cul ture	hab it a ble	or tho dox y
an nu al ly	hon our a ble	pal a ta ble
an swer a ble	ig no min y	pat ri mo ny
an ti mo ny	in ter est ing	per ish a ble
cas u al ty	in ven to ry	per emp to ry
cat er pil lar	lap i da ry	pres by te ry
cel i ba cy	lam ent a ble	prof it a ble
cer e mo ny	lit er a ry	prom is so ry
char it a ble	lit er a ture	rem e di less
dam age a ble	mat ri mo ny	sal a man der
del i ca cy	mel an chol y	sanc tu a ry
des ul to ry	mer ce na ry	sec re ta ry
dic tion a ry	mil i ta ry	sem i na ry
dil i gent ly	mis sion a ry	tes ti mo ny
em is sa ry	nec es sa ry	tol er a ble
e quit a ble	nom in a tive	tran si to ry
fash ion a ble	neg a tive ly	veg e ta ble

The accented syllable long.

A mi a ble	glo ri ous ly	mu tu al ly
co pi ous ly	hu mour ous ly	nu mer ous ly
cu li na ry	ju di ca ture	pu ri fi er
dan ger ous ly	lu mi na ry	right e ous ness
du ti ful ly	me li o rate	sta tion a ry
fa vour a ble	mo men ta ry	va ri a ble
ge ni al ly	mu sic al ly	va ri e gate

Accent on the second syllable.——The accented syllable
short.

Ab surd i ty	di min ù tive	nu mer ic al
ad ver tise ment	dis con so late	om nip o tence
ac cent u ate	dog mat ic al	om nis ci ence*
am bas sa dor	do mes ti cate	or thog ra phy
am phib i ous	e con o my	pa ren the sis
a nal y sis	em phat ic al	par tic u lar
a nat o my	ef fec tu ai	pen in su la
a non y mous	ex per i ment	pe nul ti mate
a poc a lypse	ex trav a gant	phi los o phy
a pos tro phe	e vent u ate	po lit ic al
ar ith me tic	fas tid i ous	po lyg a my
ar tic u late	fe roc i ty	pre sump tu ous
ar tif i cer	fer til i ty	re al i ty
as par a gus	fi del i ty	re cep ta cle
as tron o mer	ha bit u al	re cip ro cal
bar bar i ty	ge og ra phy	re gen er ate
be nev o lent	hy poth e sis	ri dic u lous
bi og ra phy†	i dol a ter†	rhe tor ic al
ca lam i ty	im pris on ment	sim plic i ty
ca pac i ty	in def i nite	sin cer i ty
ca tas tro phe	in dus tri ous	so lic it ous
cir cum fer ence	in hab it ant	tu mul tu ous
com mend a ble	in tem per ance	ty ran nic al
com mis er ate	lo quac i ty	un gen er ous
con sid er ate	mag nan i mous	un man ner ly
de bil i tate	me chan ic al	un nat ur al
de gen er ate	mor tal i ty	un pop u lar
de nom in ate	my thol o gy	vi cis si tude
di ag on al†	no bil i ty	vo lup tu ous

† *i* long.   * *ci* like *she.*

The accented syllable long.

b bre vi ate	e lu ci date	in de cen cy
b ste mi ous	en co mi um	in fe ri or
bu sive ly	e nu me rate	la bo ri ous
al lur ing ly	er ro ne ous	ma te ri al
a gree a ble	ex ceed ing ly	mys te ri ous
as sign a ble	ex cu sa ble	ob scu ri ty
cen so ri ous	fe lo ni ous	pos te ri or
com mo di ous	gram ma ri an	pre ca ri ous
com mu ni cant	li bra ri ant	re triev a ble
con ceiv a ble	his to ri an	sa lu bri ty
con cu pi scence	il le gal ly	schis mat i cal*
con ve ni ent	il lu mi nate	se cu ri ty
de plo ra ble	im pa tient ly	so bri e ty
de si ra ble	in ca pa ble	spon ta ne ous
dis u ni on	in cu ra ble	su pe ri or

Accent on the third syllable.——The accented syllable short.

Ad a man tine	cru ci fix ion	man u fac ture
ac a dem ic	det ri ment al	math e mat ics
ac ci dent al	dis ad van tage	om ni pres ence
ac qui es cence	dis con tin ue	op po si tion
ap pa ri tion	dis qui si tion	pen i ten tial
ap pre hen sive	e qui noc tial	pre ju di cial
av a ri cious	hor i zon tal	pre pos ses sion
co ex ist ence	im per fec tion	re qui si tion
com pre hen sive	in aus pi cious	rhet o ri cian
con de scen sion	in con sist ent	sci en tif ic†
con sci en tious	in tel lec tive	su per sti tion
cor res pon dence	in suf fi cient	un der val ue

* *ch* silent.   † *i* in first syllable long.

The accented syllable long.

Ab di ca tion	dem on stra tion	in vi ta tion
ab so lu tion	dis a gree ment	leg is la tion
ad mi ra tion	dis com pos ure	me di a tor
ad van ta geous	dis pen sa tion	mod er a tor
ac cu sa tion	ed u ca tion	ob ser va tion
af fi da vit	ef fi ca cious	op por tune ly
an no ta tor	em u la tion	os ten ta tious
ap pli ca tion	Eu ro pe an	prep a ra tion
ap pro ba tion	hy me ne al*	prov o ca tion
bar ri ca do	ig no ra mus	res ig na tion
bas ti na do	im ma-ture ly	res o lu tion
com men ta tor	in ca pa cious	sem i co lon
com pi la tion	in-cli na tion	un pol lu ted
con ver sa tion	in co he rent	vis it a tion
cul ti va tion	in ter fe rence	val u a tion

Accent on the last syllable.—The accented syllable short.

An i mad vert	mis un der stand
an te pe nult	mul ti pli cand
mis ap pre hend	nev er the less
mis rep re sent	su per in tend

SELECTIONS FROM SCRIPTURE.

My son, if sinners entice thee, consent thou not. Fools make a mock at sin.

Rejoice not when thine enemy falleth; and let not thine heart be glad when he stumbleth.

If thine enemy be hungry give him bread to eat; and if he be thirsty give him water to drink.

*y like i long.

Seest thou a man that is hasty in his words? there is more hope of a fool than of him.

Solomon, my son, know thou the GOD of thy Fathers; and serve him with a perfect heart and with a willing mind. If thou seek him, he will be found of thee; but if thou forsake him he will cast thee off forever.

He becometh poor that dealeth with a slack hand; but the hand of the diligent maketh rich.

In the multitude of words there wanteth not sin, but he that refraineth his lips is wise.

A false balance is an abomination to the Lord: but a just weight is his delight.

A fool's wrath is presently known: but a prudent man covereth shame.

Lying lips are an abomination to the Lord; but they that deal truly are his delight.

The hand of the diligent shall bear rule: but the slothful shall be under tribute.

A fool uttereth all his mind: but a wise man keepeth it in till afterwards.

If thou faint in the day of adversity, thy strength is small.

Train up a child in the way he should go: and when he is old he will not depart from it.

He that is slow to wrath is of great understanding: but he that is hasty of spirit exalteth folly.

The way of transgressors is hard.

Hatred stirreth up strife; but love covereth all sins.

7

SELECT SENTENCES.

Do to others as you wish they should do to you.

How pleasant it is to live with persons who are kind, and cheerful, and willing to oblige who never take, or keep, what does not belong to them; and who always speak the truth.

When you are told of a fault, endeavour to avoid it afterwards.

We must not do wrong because we see others do so.

Be not afraid to do what is right and proper for you to do.

Never ask other persons to do any thing for you, which you can as properly do for yourself.

As soon as you have learned to work well, try to work quick.

If we do not take pains, we must not expect to excel in any thing.

Attentive and industrious people, can always find time to do what is proper for them to do.

How comfortable it is to feel that we dearly love our parents, our brothers and sisters, and all our relations and friends; and to know that they love us, and wish to serve us, and make us happy.

Persons who desire to gain knowledge, listen to their instructers with attention and respect.

THE POWER AND GOODNESS OF GOD.

By the word of the Lord were the Heavens made; and all the host of them by the breath of his mouth. He spake, and it was done ; he commanded, and it stood fast. God said, Let there be light: and there was light. Every good gift, and every perfect gift is from above, and cometh down from the Father of Lights.

Who is like unto thee, O Lord, who is like unto thee, glorious in holiness, fearful in praises, doing wonders. Thine, O Lord, is the greatness, and the power, and the glory, and the victory, and the majesty. The eyes of all wait on thee ; thou givest them their meat in due season. Thou openest thy hand and satisfiest the desire of every living thing. Thou makest the out-goings of the morning and evening to rejoice. Thou visitest the earth, and waterest it. Thou waterest the ridges thereof abundantly ; thou settlest the furrows thereof : thou makest it soft with showers ; thou blessest the springing thereof. Thou crownest the year with thy goodness ; and thy paths drop fatness. They drop upon the pastures of the wilderness ; and the little hills rejoice on every side. The pastures are clothed with flocks ; the valleys also are covered with corn.

O that men would praise the Lord for his goodness, and for his wonderful works to the children of men.

CHAPTER XIX.
Words of Five Syllables.

Accent on the first syllable.—The accented syllable short.

Ap pli ca to ry
cus tom a ri ly
ded i ca to ry
ex pi a to ry
fig u ra tive ly
lab o ra to ry
nec es sa ri ly

ob li ga to ry
or di na ri ly
pol y syl la ble
sec ond a ri ly
spir it u al ly
sup pli ca to ry
vol un ta ri ly

Accent on the second syllable.—The accented syllable short.

A bom in a ble
a poth e ca ry
be nev o lent ly
con fec tion a ry
con sid er a ble
con tin u al ly
de pos i to ry
de clam a to ry
dis hon our a ble
dis in ter est ed
em phat ic al ly
ex plan a to ry
ex tem po ra ry
fan tas tic al ly
gram mat ic al ly
ha bit u al ly

im ag in a ry
im prac tic a ble
im pen i tent ly
im pet u ous ly
in com pa ra ble
in del i ca cy
in es ti ma ble
in ex o ra ble
ob ser va to ry
pre par a to ry
re pos i to ry
rhe tor ic al ly
tra di tion a ry
un char it a ble
un lim it a ble
un nec es sa ry

The accented syllable long.

Ab ste mi ous ness
ac cu sa to ry
cen so ri ous ness
com mu ni ca tive
ex pe ri en ced
fe lo ni ous ly
gra tu i tous ly
har mo ni ous ly
he ro i cal ly
im me di ate ly
in du bi ta ble
in nu mer a ble

in va ri a ble'
in vi o la ble
la bo ri ous ly
lux u ri ant ly
ma te ri al ly
mys te ri ous ly
no to ri ous ly
ob se qui ous ly
pe cu ni a ry
re mu ner a tive
spon ta ne ous ly
vic to ri ous ly

Accent on the third syllable—The accented syllable short.

Ac a dem ic al
ac ci dent al ly
al pha bet ic al
chris ti an i ty
con tra dic to ry
cu ri os i ty
dis a bil i ty
ge o graph i cal
hor i zon tal ly
hyp o chon dri ack
hyp o crit ic al
ig no min i ous
im per cep ti ble
in ci vil i ty
in dis pen sa ble

in fi del i ty
in sig nif i cant
ir re sist i ble
lib er al i ty
man u fac to ry
prin ci pal i ty
prod i gal i ty
re ca pit u late
reg u lar i ty
sat is fac to ry
sen si bil i ty
su per an nu ate
su per cil i ous
sys tem at ic al
trig o nom e try

The accented syllable long.

Am bi gu i ty

cer e mo ni ous

con sti tu tion al

con tu me li ous

dis a gree a ble

dis o be di ence

im ma te ri al

im me mo ri al

im pro pri e ty

in con so la ble

in con ve ni ent

in de cli na ble

in ex cu sa ble

in ge nu i ty

in ter me di ate

ir re triev a ble

mis cel la ne ous

op por tu ni ty

par si mo ni ous

pres by te ri an

sen a to ri al

si mul ta ne ous*

Accent on the fourth syllable.—The accented syllable short.

Ac a de mi cian

a rith me ti cian

char ac ter is tic

cir cum fe ren tor

en thu si as tic

ex per i ment al

in ter po si tion

math e ma ti cian

mis ap pre hend ing

mis rep re sent ed

mis un der stand ing

su per in ten dent

The accented syllable long.

Ac com mo da tion

ac cu mu la tion

al le vi a tion

ar tic u la tion

com mu ni ca tion

con sid er a tion

con tin u a tion

de lib er a tion

de nom in a tor

e quiv o ca tion

ex am in a tion

in ter ro ga tion

jus tif i ca tion

mul ti pli ca tor

re com mend a tion

sig nif i ca tion

spe cif i ca tion

sub or di na tion

* *i* long.

THE CREATION.

In the beginning God created the heaven and the earth. And God said, let the earth bring forth grass, the herb yielding seed, and the fruit-tree yielding fruit after his kind, whose seed is in itself, upon the earth : and it was so. And God created great whales, and every living creature that moveth, which the waters brought forth abundantly after their kind, and every winged fowl after his kind. And God made the beast of the earth after his kind, and cattle after their kind, and every thing that creepeth upon the earth after his kind : and God saw that it was good.

And God said, let us make man in our image, after our likeness. So God created man in his own image ; in the image of God created he him ; male and female created he them. And God blessed them, and said unto them, Be fruitful, and multiply, and replenish the earth, and subdue it ; and have dominion over the fish of the sea, and over the fowl of the air, and over every living thing that moveth upon the earth.

And God saw every thing that he had made and behold it was very good.

~~~~~~~~~~~~~~~~~

Ignorant, foolish, and obstinate persons are very disagreeable to others, and unhappy in themselves.

CHAPTER XX.

Words of six, seven, and eight Syllables, properly accented.

A be ce da' ri an
ad min is tra' tor ship
al pha bet' ic al ly
an a log' ic al ly
an a lyt' ic al ly
an ti trin i ta' ri an
arch i e pis' co pal
cer e mo' ni ous ly
cir cum nav i ga' tion
com men su ra bil' i ty
con tra dic' to ri ly
di a met' ri cal ly*
dis ci plin a' ri an
dis ad van ta' geous ly
dis in gen' u ous ness
dis in' ter est ed ness
dis o be' di ent ly
dis qual i fi ca' tion
ec cles i as' tic al
em ble mat' ic al ly
et y mo log' ic al
ex em plif i ca' tion
ex per i ment' al ly
ex tem po ra' ne ous
ge ne a log' ic al
fa mil i ar' i ty

lat i tu di na' ri an
im pos si bil' i ty
im ma te ri al' i ty
im mu ta bil' i ty
in com bus ti bil' i ty
in com men su ra bil' i ty
in com pat i bil' i ty
in con sid' er ate ly
in con ve' ni ent ly
in cor rup ti bil' i ty
in di vis i bil' i ty
in fal li bil' i ty
in stru men tal' i ty
math e mat' ic al ly
mer i to' ri ous ly
per son if i ca' tion
plen i po ten' tia ry
pre des ti na' ri an
rec om mend' a to ry
su per an' nu a ted
su per cil' i ous ness
su per nu' me ra ry
the o log' ic al ly
un in tel' li gi ble
un rea' son a ble ness
val e tu di na' ri an

* *i* in first syllable long.

WISDOM AND UNDERSTANDING.

My son, if thou wilt receive my words, and hide my commandments with thee, so that thou incline thine ear unto wisdom, and apply thine heart to understanding; yea, if thou criest after knowledge, and liftest up thy voice for understanding; if thou seekest her as silver, and searchest for her as for hid treasures; then shalt thou understand the fear of the Lord, and find the knowledge of God. For the Lord giveth wisdom : out of his mouth cometh knowledge and understanding.

Let thine heart retain my words : keep my commandments and live. Get wisdom, get understanding : forget it not : neither decline from the words of my mouth. Forsake her not, and she shall preserve thee : love her, and she shall keep thee.

Happy is the man that findeth wisdom, and the man that getteth understanding. For the merchandise of it is better than the merchandise of silver, and the gain thereof than fine gold. She is more precious than rubies ; and all the things thou canst desire are not to be compared unto her. Length of days is in her right hand : and in her left, riches and honour. Her ways are ways of pleasantness, and all her paths are peace.

CHAPTER XXI.

Irregular Words.

Spelled	Pronounced	Spelled	Pronounced
A gain	a gen'	flam beau	flam' bo
a gainst	a genst'	gaol	jale
aisle	ile	hei nous	ha' nus
a ny	en' ne	isl and	ile' and
a pron	a' purn	i ron	i' urn
bat teau	bat to'	ma ny	men' ny
beaux	boze	o cean	o' shun
bu reau	bu ro'	phthis ic	tiz' ik
bu ry	ber' ry	pret ty	prit' ty
bu ri al	ber' re al	su gar	shoo' gur
bu sy	biz' ze	sure	shure
busi ness	biz' ness	vis count	vi' count
colo nel	cur' nel	vict uals	vit' tlz
corps	core	wom en	wim' in
ew er	yu' ur	yes	yis

TRUTH.

Consider well before you make a promise. If you say you will do a thing, and do it not, you will tell a lie; and who then will trust or, believe you? No persons are trusted, or believed, but those who keep their promises, and speak the truth. When you have done wrong do not deny it. It is very sinful to tell lies. God himself has said that we must not lie: that he abhors liars and will punish them.

DIVINE PROVIDENCE.

The glorious sun is set in the west; the night-dews fall; and the air which was sultry becomes cool. The flowers fold up their coloured leaves; they fold themselves up, and hang their heads on their slender stalks. The chickens are gathered under the wing of the hen, and are at rest; the hen herself is at rest also. The little birds have ceased their warbling; they are asleep on the boughs, each one with his head beneath his wing. There is no murmur of bees around the hive or among the honeyed woodbines; they have done their work, and they lie close in their waxen cells. The sheep are at rest upon their soft fleeces, and their loud bleating is no more heard among the hills. There is no sound of a number of voices, or of children at play, or the trampling of busy feet. The

smith's hammer is not heard upon the anvil;
nor the harsh saw of the carpenter. All men
are stretched on their quiet beds; and the
child sleeps upon the breast of its mother.
Darkness is spread over the skies, and darkness is upon the ground; every eye is shut,
and every hand is still.

Who takes care of all people when they
are sunk in sleep; when they cannot defend
themselves, nor see if danger approaches?
There is an eye that never sleeps; there is
an eye that sees in the dark night, as well as
in the bright sunshine. When there is no
light of the sun, nor of the moon; when there
is no lamp in the house, nor any little star
twinkling through the thick clouds; that eye
sees every where, in all places, and watches
continually over all the families of the earth.
The eye, that sleeps not, is God's; his hand is
always stretched out over us. He made
sleep to refresh us when we are weary. As
the mother moves about the house with her
finger on her lips, and stills every little noise
that her infant be not disturbed; as she draws
the curtains around its bed, and shuts out the
light from its tender eyes; so God draws the
curtains of darkness around us; so he makes
all things to be hushed and still, that his large
family may sleep in peace.

Labourers spent with toil, and young children, and every little humming insect, sleep
quietly, for God watches over you. You may

sleep, for he never sleeps ; you may close your eyes in safety, for his eye is always open to protect you. When the darkness is passed away, and the beams of the morning sun strike through your eyelids, begin the day with praising God, who has taken care of you through the night. Let his praise be in our hearts, when we lie down ; let his praise be on our lips, when we awake.

NEGLIGENCE.

Children are apt to think, that a few minutes added to their diversions can make no difference ; and minutes slip away insensibly into a quarter of an hour : their play becomes more interesting, the game is nearly concluded, or the kite will be down, it is a pity to stop its flight ; a race will shortly be determined, or some such reason prevails, till the time is elapsed in which their business should have been attended to ; and they are left to bewail, in sorrow and regret, the folly of their negligence. It would be more prudent, therefore, at first, to secure essentials, and do what is necessary, before they begin to engage in those diversions, which, however laudable in their proper season, may frequently insnare them into an errour, and subject them to severe punishment.

8

ADVICE TO CHILDREN.

Listen to the affectionate counsels of your parents; treasure up their precepts; respect their riper judgment; and enjoy, with gratitude and delight, the advantages resulting from their society. Bind to your bosom, by the most endearing ties, your brothers and sisters; cherish them as your best companions, through the variegated journey of life; and suffer no jealousies and contentions to interrupt the harmony, which should ever reign among you.

~~~~~~~~~~~

The honour which children are required to give to their father and mother includes in it, love, reverence, obedience, and relief. It is usual with Providence to return, in kind, men's disobedience to their parents.

INDUSTRY AND SLOTH.

Love not sleep, lest thou come to poverty; open thine eyes, and thou shalt be satisfied with bread. Go to the ant, thou sluggard, consider her ways, and be wise : which having no guide, overseer, or ruler, provideth her meat in the summer and gathereth her food in the harvest. How long wilt thou sleep, O sluggard? when wilt thou arise out of thy sleep? Yet a little sleep, a little slumber, a little folding of the hands to sleep : so shall thy poverty come as one that travelleth, and thy want as an armed man.

I went by the field of the slothful, and by the vineyard of the man void of understanding. And lo, it was all grown over with thorns, and nettles had covered the face thereof, and the stone wall thereof was thrown down. Then I saw, and considered it well : I looked upon it and received instruction.

Be thou diligent to know the state of thy flocks, and look well to thy herds. He that tilleth his land shall have plenty of bread; but he that followeth vain persons shall have poverty enough.

We beseech you, brethren, that ye study to do your own business, and to work with your own hands, as we commanded you.

Whatsoever thine hand findeth to do, do it with thy might ; for there is no work, nor device, nor knowledge, nor wisdom, in the grave whither thou goest.

THE HUMMING BIRD.

The humming-bird , is the most beautiful
and inoffensive of all birds. Of this charming
little animal, there are six or seven varieties,
from the size of a small wren, down to that of
an humble bee. One would not readily suppose that there existed any birds so very small,
and yet so completely furnished with bill,
feathers, wings and intestines, exactly like
those of the largest kind. Birds not so big
as the end of one's little finger, would proba-
bly be thought mere creatures of imagination,
were they not seen in great numbers, in the
warm latitudes of America, sporting in the
fields from flower to flower, and extracting
sweets with their little bills.

The smallest humming-bird is about the
size of a hazel-nut. The feathers on its wings
and tail are black; but those on its body and

under its wings, are of a greenish brown, with a fine red cast or gloss, which no silk cr velvet can imitate. It has a small crest on its head, green at the bottom, and as it were gilded at the top; and which sparkles in the sun, like a little star in the middle of its forehead. The bill is black, straight, slender, and of the length of a pin.

As soon as the sun is risen, the humming-birds of different kinds, are seen fluttering about the flowers, without ever lighting upon them. Their wings are in such rapid motion, that it is impossible to discern their colours, except by their glittering. They are never still but continually in motion, visiting flower after flower, and extracting its honey as if with a kiss. For this purpose they are furnished with a forky tongue, that enters the cup of the flower, and extracts its nectared tribute. Upon this alone they subsist. The rapid motion of their wings occasions a humming sound, from whence they have their name.

The nests of these birds are also very curious. They are suspended in the air at the point of the twigs of an orange, a pomegranate or a citron tree; sometimes even in houses, if a small and convenient twig is found for the purpose. The female is the architect, while the male goes in quest of materials; such as cotton, fine moss, and the fibres of vegetables. Of these materials a nest is composed, about the size of a hen's egg cut in two ; it is admirably contrived, and warmly lined with cotton. _ There are never more than two eggs found in a nest; these are about the size of a small pea, and as white as snow, with here and there a yellow speck. The male and female sit upon the nest by turns ; but the female takes to herself the greatest share. She seldom quits the nest, except a few minutes in the morning and ev-. ening, when the dew is upon the flowers, and their honey in perfection. During this short interval, the male takes her place. The time of incubation continues twelve days ; at the end of which the young ones appear. They are at first bare ; by degrees, they are covered with down ; and at last feathers succeed, less beautiful at first than the old ones.

A gentleman in that part of America where these birds most abound, found the nest of a humming-bird, in a shed near the dwelling house ; and took it in, at a time when the young ones were fifteen or twenty days old. He placed them in a cage in his chamber window to be amused with their sportive flutterings ; but he was soon surprised to see the old ones come and feed their brood regularly every hour of the day. By this means they themselves grew so tame, that they seldom quitted the chamber ; and without any constraint came to live with their young ones. All four frequently perched upon their master's hand, chirping as if they had been at liberty abroad. He fed them with a very fine clear paste, made of wine, biscuit, and sugar. They thrust their tongues into this paste, till they were satisfied, and then fluttered and chirped about the room. This lovely little family had possession of the chamber, and flew in and out just as they thought proper; but were very attentive to the voice of their master, when he called them. In this manner they lived with him about six months: but at the time when he expected to see a new colony formed, he unfortunately forgot to tie up their cage to the ceiling at night, to preserve them from the rats, and he found in the morning, to his great mortification, that they were all devoured,

THE FOUR SEASONS.

Who is this beautiful virgin that approaches, clothed in a robe of light green? She has a garland of flowers on her head, and flowers spring up wherever she sets her foot. The snow which covered the fields, and the ice which was in the rivers, melt away when she breathes upon them. The young lambs frisk about her, and the birds warble in their little throats to welcome her coming; and when they see her, they begin to choose their mates, and to build their nests. Youths and

maidens, have you seen this beautiful virgin?
If you have, tell me who she is, and what is
her name.

Who is this that comes from the south,
thinly clad in a light transparent garment?
Her breath is hot and sultry; she seeks the
refreshment of the cool shade ; she seeks
the clear streams, the crystal brooks, to
bathe her languid limbs.   The brooks and
rivulets fly from her, and are dried up at her
approach.   She cools her parched lips with
berries, and the grateful acid of fruits, the
seedy melon, the sharp apple, and the red
pulp of the juicy cherry, which are scattered
plentifully around her.   The tanned hay-
makers welcome her coming ; and the sheep-
shearer, who clips the fleeces of his flock
with his sounding shears.   When she comes,
let me lie under the thick shade of a spreading beech-tree ; let me walk with her in the
early morning, when the dew is yet upon the
grass ; let me wander with her in the soft
twilight, when the shepherd shuts his fold,
and the star of evening appears.   Who is she
that comes from the south? Youths and maidens, tell me if you know, who is she, and
what is her name.

Who is he that with sober pace, steals upon us unawares? His garments are red with

the blood of the grape, and his temples are bound with a sheaf of ripe wheat. His hair is thin, and begins to fall, and the auburn is mixed with mournful gray. He shakes the brown nuts from the tree. He winds the horn, and calls the hunters to their sports. The gun sounds. The trembling partridge, and the beautiful pheasant flutter, bleeding in the air, and fall dead at the sportsman's feet. Who is he that is crowned with the wheat-sheaf? Youths and maidens, tell me if you know, who is he, and what is his name.

Who is he that comes from the north, clothed in fur and warm wool? He wraps his cloak close about him. His head is bald ; his beard is made of sharp icicles. He loves the blazing fire, high piled upon the hearth. He binds skates to his feet, and skims over the frozen lakes. His breath is piercing and cold, and no little flower dares to peep above the surface of the ground, when he is by. Whatever he touches turns to ice. If he were to strike you with his cold hand, you would be quite stiff, and dead, like a piece of marble. Youths and maidens, do you see him? He is coming fast upon us, and soon he will be here. Tell me, if you know, who is he and what is his name.

COVETOUSNESS,

Thou shalt not covet any thing that is thy neighbour's. If riches increase, set not thy heart upon them. I know there is no good in them, but for a man to rejoice, and to do good in his life. He that hateth covetousness shall prolong his days. He that loveth silver shall not be satisfied therewith; nor he that loveth abundance, with increase.

Lay not up for yourselves treasures upon earth, where moth and rust doth corrupt, and where thieves break through and steal: but lay up for yourselves, treasures in heaven, where neither moth nor rust doth corrupt, and where thieves do not break through nor steal. For where your treasure is, there will your heart be also.

Give me neither poverty nor riches; feed me with food convenient for me : lest I be full and deny thee, and say, Who is the Lord? or lest I be poor and steal, and take the name of my God in vain.

THE FLOOD.

And God looked upon the earth, and behold, it was corrupt: for all flesh had corrupted his way upon the earth. And God said unto Noah, the end of all flesh is come before me ; for the earth is filled with violence through them; and behold I will destroy them with the earth.

. Make thee an ark of gopherwood : rooms shalt thou make in the ark, and shalt pitch it within and without with pitch. The length of the ark shall be three hundred cubits, the breadth of it fifty cubits, and the height of it thirty cubits. A window shalt thou make in the ark, and the door of the ark shalt thou set in the side thereof; with lower, second, and third stories shalt thou make it.

And come thou and all thy house into the ark; for thee have I seen righteous before me in this generation. Of every clean beast thou shalt take to thee by sevens, the male and his female; and of beasts that are not clean by two, the male and his female; of fowls also of the air by sevens, the male and the female, to keep seed alive upon the face of the earth. And take unto thee of all food that is eaten, and it shall be for food for thee and for them. And Noah did according to all that the Lord commanded him.

And Noah went in, and his sons, and his wife, and his sons' wives with him into the ark. Of clean beasts. and of beasts that are not clean, and of fowls, and of every thing that creepeth upon the earth, there went in two and two unto Noah into the ark. And the Lord shut him in.

In the six hundredth year of Noah's life, in the second month, in the seventeenth day of the month, were all the fountains of the great deep broken up, and all the windows of Heaven were opened. And the rain was upon the earth forty days and forty nights. And the waters increased and bare up the ark, and it was lifted up above the earth. And the waters prevailed exceedingly upon the earth, and the ark went upon the face of the waters. Fifteen cubits upward did the waters prevail, and the mountains were covered. And all flesh died that moved upon the earth ; all in whose nostrils was the breath of life ; all that was in the dry land died. And Noah only remained alive, and they that were with him in the ark.

And after the end of an hundred and fifty days the waters were abated. And the ark rested upon the mountains of Ararat. And the waters decreased continually ; and in the tenth month, on the first day of the month, were the tops of the mountains seen. And in the six hundredth and first year, in the second month, and on the seven and twentieth day of the month was the earth dried.

And God spake unto Noah, saying, Go forth of the ark. And Noah went forth, and his sons, and his wife, and his sons' wives with him ; every beast, every creeping thing, and every fowl, and whatsoever creepeth upon the earth, after their kinds, went forth out of the ark.

CHAPTER XXII.

NAMES OF MEN.

Aa' ron
A' bel
A bi' el
A bi' jah
Ab' ner
A' bra ham
Ad' am
Al' bert
Al' len
Al ex an' der
Al' fred
Al phe' us
A' mos
An' drew
An' tho ny
A pol' los
A' ri el
Ar' te mas
Ar' thur
Ben' ja min
Ca' leb
Cal' vin
Charles
Chris' to pher
Cor ne' li us
Cy' rus
Dan' i el
Da' vid
Eb en e' zer

E' ber
Ed' mund
Ed' ward
Ed' gar
El' dad
E le a' zer
E' li
E li' as
E li e' zer
El' mer
E li' sha
E liph' a let
E' noch
E' nos
E' phra im
E ze' ki el
Ez' ra
Fran' cis
Fred' er ic
George
Gid' e on
Gil' bert
Hen' ry
Hor' ace
Ho ra' tio
Hez e ki' ah
I' ra
I' saac
Is' ra el

I sai' ah*
James
Ja' cob
Jer e mi' ah
Jes' se
Job
Jo' el
John
Jo' nas
Jo' seph
Josh' u a
Jon' a than
Lem' u el
Leon' ard
Le' vi
Lew' is
Lot
Luke
Lu' ther
Mat' thew
Mo' ses
Na' than
Na than' i el
Ne he mi' ah
Nich' o las
No' ah
O ba di' ah
Ol' i ver
Pe' ter

* I sa' yah.

9

Paul
Pel a ti' ah
Phil' ip
Phin' e has
Reu' ben
Rich' ard
Rob' ert
Ru' fus
Sal' mon
Sam' son

Sam'. u el
Saul
Seth
Sheb' na
Shu' ba el
Sim' e on
Si' mon
Sol' o mon
Ste' phen
Si' las

The' o dore
The oph' i lus
Thom',as
Tim' o thy
U' ri
U ri' ah
Wâl' ter
Will' iám
Zech a ri' ah
Ze rub' bá bel

NAMES OF WOMEN.

Ăb' i gail
A man' da
A me' li a
Ann
An' na
As' e nath
Cath'a rine
Car' o line
Chlo' e
Cla ris' sa
Deb' o rah
De' li a
Di' nah
Dor' cas
Dor' o thy
El' ea nor
E li' za
E liz' a beth
El mi' ra
El vi' ra
Em' ma

Em' i ly
Esth' er
Em me line
Fran' ces
Han' nah
Har' ri et
Hel' en
Hen ri et' ta
Hul' dah
Is' a bel
Jane
Ju' li a
Ju li an' na
Lou i' sat
Lo' is
Lu' ci a
Lu' cy
Lyd' i a
Lu cin' da
Lu cre' tia
Ma' rah

Mar' ga ret
Mar' tha
Ma ri' a
Ma' ry
Ma til' da
Nan' cy
Na o' mi
Pa' tience
Phe' be
Pris cil' la
Pru' dence
Ra' chel
Re bec' ca
Rho' da
Ruth
Sa lo' me
Sa' rah
So phi' a
Su' san
Su san' nah
Tab' i tha

† *i* like *e* long.

CHAPTER XXIII.

Names of Places.

IN EUROPE.

Am' ster dam	Glas' gow	Pe' ters burg
Aus' tri a	Greece	Po' land
Ba va' ri a	Hague	Ro me ra' ni a
Berne	Hol' land	Pōr' tu gal
Bo he' mi a	Hŭn' ga ry	Prague
Bra gan' za	Ice' land	Prus' sia
Brus' sels	Ire' land	Ra gu' sa
Ca' diz	It' a ly	Rome
Co pen ha' gen	Lap' land	Rus' sia
Cor' si ca	Leg' born	Sar din' i a
Den' mark	Lis' bon	Sax' o ny
Dub' lin	Lon' don	Scot'land
Eng' land	Mad rid'	Sic' i ly
Ed' in burgh	Mu' nich	Spain
Fin' land	Mo ra' vi a	Swe' den
Flor' ence	Mos' cow	Swit' zer land
France	Na' ples	Tus' ca ny
Gen e' va	Nеth' er lands	Ven' ice
Gen' o a	Nor' way	Vi en' na
Ger' ma ny	Pa ler' mo	Wales
Gib râl' tar	Par' is	Zeal' and

IN ASIA.

A ra' bi a	Chi' na	Mec' ca
Ar me' ni a	Hin doos' tan	Pe' kin
Bom' bay	In'di a	Per' si a
Cal cut' ta	Ja pan'	Tar' ta ry
Can' ton	Ma dras'	Thi' bet

IN AFRICA,

A bys sin' i a	E' gypt	Mo roc' co
Al ex an' dri a	E thi o' pi a	Nu' bi a
Al giērs'	Fez	Sen e gâl'
Bar' ba ry	Gam' bi a	Trip' o li
Cai' ro	Guin' ea	Tu' nis

IN AMERICA.

Accent on the first syllable,

Âl ba ny	Fal mouth	Lou is ville
An do ver	Flor i da	Maine
Bâl ti more	Frank fort	Ma ry land
Ban gor	Frye burg	Mex i co
Ben ning ton	George town	Mid dle bu ry
Berk shire	Geor gi a	Mid dle sex
Bos ton	Glouces ter	Natch es
'Brat tle borough	Hal i fax	Nash ville
Bruns wick	Hâl lo well	New ark
Bur ling ton	Hamp den	New bern
Cām bridge	Han o ver	New cas tle
Charles town	Hart ford	New bu ry port
Chesh ire	Ha ver hill	Ne vis
Chi li (*Che'le*)	James town	Nor ridge wock
Con cord	Keene	North field
Cu ba	Kings ton	Or le ans
Cu ma na	Knox ville	Pe ters burg
Cum ber land	Lab ra dor	Pitts burg
Dan ville	Lan cas ter	Pitts field
Dart mouth	Lan sin burg	Plym outh
Deer field	Leb a non	Port land
Del a ware	Leices ter	Ports mouth
East port	Lex ing ton	Prince ton
Ex e ter	Liv er pool	Prov i dence

Ran dolph
Read ing
Rich mond
Rock ing ham
Rut land
Sâ co
Sâl*i*s bu ry
Sa lem
Scнuy lėr
Shrews bu ry

Smith field
Spring field
Suf folk
Tàun ton
Tren ton
Wâl pole
Wâl tham
War ren*
Wash ing ton*
West min ster

Wheel ing
Will iams burg
Will iams town
Wil ming ton
Wind sor
Wood stock
Worces ter
York
York town

Accent on the second syllable.

A mer i ca
An guil la
An nap o lis
An ti gua†
Au gus ta
Ba ha ma
Bar ba does
Bar bu da
Ber mu da
Cas tine†
Co lum bi a
Con nect i cut
Co os
Ca rac cas
De troit
Do min go
Eu sta tia
Gre na da
Ha van na
Hen lo pen

Hon du ras
Ja mai ca
Kas kas ki as
Ken tuc ky
Ma chi as
Man hat tan
Mi am i
Mis sou ri
Mo bile†
Mont pe lier
Mus kin gum
Nan tuck et
New Eng land
New Hamp shire
New Ha ven
New Jer sey
New Or le ans
New York
Ni ag a ra
North amp ton

O hi o
O nei da
Pa tap sco
Paw tuck et
Pa tux et
Pe nob scot
Pe ru
R*h*ode is land‡
San dus ky
Sa van nab
Se bas ti cook
Scнe nec ta dy
To ba go
Ver mont
Ver gen*n*es
Vir gin i a
West In dies
West hamp ton
Wâ chu sett
Wis cas set

* *a* like *o* short. † *i* like *e* long. ‡ *s* silent.
9*

Accent on the third syllable,

Ac a pul co	Guâ da lôupe	Nic a rà gua
Al be marle	Gua ti ma la	Pat a go ni a
Al a bà ma	Il li nois	Pen sa co la
Au gus tine*	In di a na	Penn syl va ni a
Cal i for ni a	Ken ne beck	Phil a del phi a
Car tha ge na	Mar ble head	Pon char train
Chil i co the	Ma ri et ta	Por to bel lo
Cher o kee	Mar ti ni co*	Por to ri co*
Cin cin nà ti	Mas sa chu setts	Sar a to ga
Dem a ra ra	Mis sis sip pi	Sur i nam
Dom i ni co*	Mont ser rat	Ten nes see
Gen nes see	Mont re âl	Trin i dad

*i like e long.

A CHILD'S HYMN OF PRAISE.

I THANK the goodness and the grace,
  Which on my birth have smil'd,
And made me in these latter days,
  A happy English child.

I was not born, as thousands are,
  Where God was never known;
And taught to pray a useless prayer
  To blocks of wood and stone.

I was not born a little slave,
  To labour in the sun,
And wish I were but in the grave,
  And all my labour done!

I was not born without a home,
  Or in some broken shed ;
A gipsy baby, taught to roam,
  And steal my daily bread.

My God, I thank thee, thou hast plann'd
  A better lot for me,
And plac'd me in this happy land,
  Where I may hear of thee.

ENCOURAGEMENT FOR LITTLE CHILDREN.

God is so good, that he will hear
  Whenever children humbly pray.
He always lends a gracious ear
  To what the youngest child can say.

His own most holy Book declares
  He loves good little children well ;
And that he listens to their prayers,
  Just as a tender father will.

He loves to hear an infant tongue
  Thank him for all his mercies given ;
And when by babes his praise is sung,
  Their cheerful songs are heard in heaven.

Come then, dear children, trust his word,
  And seek him for your friend and guide :
Your little voices will be heard,
  And you shall never be denied.

AN EVENING HYMN FOR A LITTLE FAMILY.

Now condescend, Almighty King,
  To bless this little throng ;
And kindly listen while we sing
  Our pleasant evening song.

We come to own the Power Divine,
  That watches o'er our days ;
For this our feeble voices join
  In hymns of cheerful praise.

Before the sacred footstool, see,
  We bend in humble prayer,
A happy little family,
  To ask thy tender care.

May we in safety sleep to-night,
  From every danger free ;
Because the darkness and the light
  Are both alike to thee.

And when the rising sun displays
  His cheerful beams abroad,
Then shall our morning hymns of praise
  Declare thy goodness, Lord.

Brothers and sisters, hand in hand,
  Our lips together move ;
Then smile upon this little band,
  And join our hearts in love.

THE WINTER'S DAY.

When raging storms deform the air,
  And clouds of snow descend ;
And the wide landscape, bright and fair,
  No deepen'd colours blend ;

When biting frost rides on the wind,
  Bleak from the north and east,
And wealth is at its ease reclin'd,
  Prepar'd to laugh or feast ;

When the poor trav'ller treads the plain,
  All dubious of his way,
And crawls with night-increasing pain,
  And dreads the parting day ;

When poverty, in vile attire,
  Shrinks from the biting blast,
Or hovers o'er the pigmy fire,
  And fears it will not last ;

When the fond mother hugs her child
  Still closer to her breast ;
And the poor infant, frost-beguil'd,
  Scarce feels that it is press'd ;—

Then let your bounteous hand extend
  Its blessings to the poor ;
Nor spurn the wretched, when they bend,
  All suppliant, at your door.

THE FALL OF THE LEAF.

See the leaves around us falling,
  Dry and withered to the ground;
Thus to thoughtless mortals calling,
  In a sad and solemn sound:

" Sons of Adam, (once in Eden,
  When like us, he blighted fell,)
Hear the lecture we are reading;
  'Tis alas! the truth we tell.

Virgins, much, too much presuming
  On your boasted white and red;
View us, late in beauty blooming,
  Numbered now among the dead.

Youths, though yet no losses grieve you,
  Gay in health, and many a grace;
Let not cloudless skies deceive you;
  Summer gives to autumn place.

Yearly in our course returning,
  Messengers of shortest stay
Thus we preach this truth concerning,
  Heav'n and Earth shall pass away.

On the tree of life eternal,
  Man, let all thy hopes be staid;
Which alone, forever vernal,
  Bears a leaf that shall not fade."

CHAPTER XXIV.

Words alike in sound, but different in spelling and signification.

Ale, malt liquor.

Ail, a disease.

Air, wind.

Heir, one who inherits.

E'er, *contraction for* ever.

Ere, before.

All, every one.

Awl, an instrument.

Al' ter, to change.

Al' tar, for sacrifice.

An' ker, a liquid measure.

An' chor, a heavy iron to hold a ship.

Ark, a chest.

Arc, an arch.

Au' ger, a tool.

Au' gur, one who foretells.

As' cent, steepness.

As' sent, agreement.

Bad, ill, vicious.

Bade, *past time of* bid.

Bale, a package of goods

Bail, surety.

Bate, to lessen,

Bait, temptation.

Bawl, to cry aloud.

Ball, any round thing.

Bare, naked.

Bear, to suffer ; a beast.

Base, vile.

Bass, in music.

Be, to exist.

Bee, an insect.

Beech, a kind of tree.

Beach, a shore.

Beet, a plant.

Beat, to strike.

Beer, a kind of liquor.

Bier, a carriage for the dead.

Bell, a sounding vessel.

Belle, a gay lady.

Ber' ry, a small fruit.

Bu' ry, to inter the dead.

Bin, a place for corn.

Been, *part. of* to be.

Bite, to wound.

Bight, the doubling of a rope.

Blue, a colour.

Blew, *past time of* blow.

Bore, to make holes.

Boar, a male swine.

Bur' row, a rabbit hole.

Bor' ough, a corpora-tion.

Bou*gh*, a branch.
Bow, to bend.
   B*ow*, to shoot with.
   Beau, a gay fellow.
Bred, brought up.
Bread, food made of meal.
By, a particle.
Buy, to purchase.
Butt, to strike like a ram.
But, except.
   Cane, a staff.
   Cain, a man's name. [en
Cal' *en* der, to smooth lin-
Cal' en dar, an almanack.
   Caul, a membrane.
   Call, to cry out.
Can' non, a large gun.
Can' on, a rule.
   Can' vas, coarse cloth.
   Can' vass, to examine.
Seal, to fasten with a seal;
   the sea calf.
Ceil, to make a ceiling.
   Seal' ing, setting a seal.
   Ceil' ing, of a room.
Cen' ser, a pan for incense.
Cen' sor, a reformer.
   Cell, a hut.
   Sell, to dispose of.
Cent, a piece of money.
Scent, a smell.
Sent, did send.
   Cen' tu ry, 100 years.
   Cen' tau ry, an herb.

Ces' sion, resignation.
Ses' sion, act of setting.
   C*h*ol' er, wrath.
   Col' lar, for the neck.
Chop, to cut.
Chap, a beast's jaw.
   C*h*ord, in music.
   Cord, a small rope.
Cite, to summon.
Si*gh*t, seeing.
Site, situation.
   Cliff, a steep rock.
   Clef, a term in music.
Co*a*rse, not fine.
Co*u*rse, a race.
Corse, a dead body.
   Clime, a climate.
   Clim*b*, to mount up.
Com'ple ment, full number.
Com' pli ment, act of ci-
   vility.
   Co quet, (*co ket'*) to
   deceive in love.
   Co quette', an airy girl.
Core, the inner part.
Corps, a body of soldiers
   Cous' in, a relation.
   Coz' *en*, to cheat.
Cru' el, inhuman,
Crew' el, worsted thread
   Sig' net, a seal.
   Cyg'net, a young swan.
Dam, a mother.
Dam*n*, to condemn.

Deer, an animal.
Dear, costly, beloved.
De mean', to behave.
De mesne', a freehold.
Due, owing.
Dew, on the grass.
Doe, a female deer.
Dough, unbaked bread.
Dun, a colour.
Done, performed,
Ex' er cise, to practise.
Ex' or cise, to cast out evil spirits.
I, myself.
Eye, the organ of sight.
Fane, a temple.
Fain, gladly.
Feign, to dissemble.
Faint, feeble.
Feint, a false march.
Fare, food, hire.
Fair, comely.
Feet, of the body.
Feat, an action.
Fel'loe, the circumference of a wheel.
Fel' low, an associate.
Fir, a tree.
Fur, a skin.
Flee, to run away.
Flea, an insect.
Flue, pipe of an oven.
Flew, did fly.

Flour, meal.
Flow' er, a blossom.
Fore, anteriour.
Four, in number.
Forth, forward, onward.
Fourth, in number.
Foul, filthy.
Fowl, a bird.
Freeze, to congeal.
Frieze, coarse cloth.
Gate, a large door.
Gait, manner of walking
Gilt, overlaid with gold.
Guilt, crime.
Grate, to rub small.
Great, large.   [with.
Gra' ter, a thing to grate
Great' er, larger.
Grown, increased.
Groan, to sigh.
Hale, sound, healthy.
Hail, to salute, frozen drops of rain.
Haul, to draw by force.
Hall, a large room.
Hart, a beast.
Heart, the seat of life.
Hare, an animal.
Hair, of the head.
Heel, part of the foot.
Heal, to cure.
Herd, a drove.
Heard, did hear.

10

Here, in this place.
Hear, to hearken..
Him, that man.
Hymn, a sacred song.
Hire, wages.
High' er, further up.
Hole. a cavity.
Whole, the total.
Hue, a colour.
Hugh, a man's name.
Hew, to cut.
In, within.
Inn, a tavern.
Ile, } an alley in a
Aisle, } church,
Isle, an island.
In dite', to compose.
In dict', to prosecute.
Key, a tool to open a lock.
Quay (*kee*) a wharf.
Kill, to slay.
Kiln, of bricks.
Lade, to load, to dip.
Laid, placed, did lay.
Lane, a narrow passage.
Lain, *participle of* to lie.
Leek, a plant.
Leak, to let water in or
    out.
Led, did lead.
Lead, a heavy metal.
Leave, permission.
Lieve, willingly.
Les' sen, to diminish.

Les' son, a reading.
Li' ar, one who tells lies.
Lyre, a harp.
Limb, part of the body.
Limn, to paint.
Lo, behold.
Low, not high.
Lone, solitary.
Loan, a thing lent.
Made, finished.   [man
Maid, an unmarried wo-
Male, the he kind.
Mail, armour, packet
    of letters.
Mane, long hair on the
    neck of a horse.
Main, principal.
Mare, a female horse.
May' or, a magistrate.
Man' ner, mode, custom.
Man' or, a lordship.
Man' tle, a kind of
    cloak.
Man' tel, work raised
    before a chimney.
Mar' shal, to arrange.
Mar' tial, warlike.
Maze, a labyrinth.
Maize, corn.
Mean, base, to intend.
Mien, air, look.
Mete, to measure.
Meet, to come together.
Meat, flesh.

Met' tle, briskness. [iron.

Met' al, gold, silver, or

  Mi' ner, one who digs

    mines.

  Mi' nor, one under age.

Mite, a small insect.

Might, power.

  Moan, to lament.

  Mown, cut down.

Mote, a particle of dust.

Moat, a ditch.

  More, greater. [mows.

  Mow' er, one who

Nag, a gay horse.

Knag, a knot in wood.

  Nave, part of a wheel.

  Knave, a rogue.

Naught, bad, wicked.

Nought, nothing.

  Nay, no.

  Neigh, voice of a horse.

Need, want.

Knead, to make dough.

  New, not old.

  Knew, did know.

Night, time of darkness.

Knight, a title of honour.

  Nit, the egg of a louse.

  Knit, to unite, to close.

No, word of denial.

Know, to be informed.

  Not, denying.

  Knot, hard place in

    wood.

Nun, a religious woman.

None, not any. [rated.

  Ore, metal not sepa-

  Oar, an instrument to

    row with. [over.

  O'er, *contraction of*

Oh, alas.

Owe, to be indebted.

  Won, (*wun*) *past time*

    of win.

  One, in number.

Our, belonging to us.

*H*our, sixty minutes.

  Aught, any thing.

  Ought, obliged by duty.

Pale, wanting colour.

Pail, a wooden vessel.

Pane, a square of glass.

Pain, torment.

Pare, to cut off.

Pair, a couple.

Pear, a kind of fruit.

  Pal' let, a little bed.

  Pal' ette, a painter's

    board. [wainscot.

Pan' el, a square in a

Pan' nel, a kind of saddle.

  Peel, the outside.

  Peal, a succession of

    sudden sounds.

Peer, a nobleman.

Pier, a column.

  Peace, quiet.

  Piece, a part.

Peak, top of a hill.
Pique, a grudge.
Plane, flat surface, a [tool.
Plain, level.
Plate, a flat piece of metal.
Plait, a fold.
Place, locality.
Plaice, a kind of fish.
Plum, a kind of fruit.
Plumb, a weight.
Pole, a long stick.
Poll, the head.
Pour, to empty out.
Pore, passage of perspiraration.
Pen' cil, an instrument for writing.
Pen' sile, hanging.
Pray, to supplicate.
Prey, plunder.
Prof' it, advantage.
Proph' et, a foreteller.
Rab' bit, an animal.
Rab' bet, a joint.
Rain, falling water.
Rein, part of a bridle.
Reign, to rule.
Rap, to strike.
Wrap, to fold together.
Raze, to demolish.
Raise, to set up.
Rays, light.
Reed, a plant.
Read, to peruse.

Red, a colour.
Read, did read.
Rest, quiet.
Wrest, to force.
Rice, a plant.
Rise, origin.
Rig' ger, one who rigs.
Rig' our, severity.
Ring, to sound.
Wring, to twist.
Rite, a ceremony.
Right, just.   [wood.
Wright, an artificer in
Write, to form letters with
Rode, did ride. [a pen.
Road, a highway.
Rote, memory.
Wrote, did write [a fish.
Roe, a deer; the eggs of
Row, a rank.
Room, space.   [mour.
Rheum, thin watery hu_
Ruff, a ruffle.
Rough, not smooth.
Rye, grain.
Wry, crooked.
Sale, act of selling.
Sail, of a ship.
Seen, beheld.
Scene, part of a play.
Seine, a net for fish.
See, to behold.
Sea, the ocean.
Seed, first principle.

Cede, to resign.
Sere, withered.
Cere, to wax.
Sear, to burn.
Se'er, a prophet.
Seem, to appear.
Seam, edges sewed, a scar.
Sen' ior, elder.
Seign' or, a lord.
Sel' ler, one who sells.
Cel' lar, a place under a house.
Shore, side of a river.
Shoar, a prop.
Sheer, thin.
Shear, to cut.
Shire, a county.
Sine, a geometrical line.
Sign, a token.
Sink, to go down, a drain.
Cinque, number five on dice.
Sit, to be seated.
Cit, a citizen.
Size, bulk.
Sice, number six on dice.
Slay, to kill.
Slaie, a weaver's reed.
Sleigh, carriage used on snow.
Slight, to despise.
Sleight, dexterity.
Slow, not swift.
Sloe, a fruit.
So, thus.

Sow, to scatter seed.
Sew, to use a needle.
Sore, an ulcer.
Soar, to mount aloft.
Sole, bottom of the foot.
Soul, the spirit.
Stare, to gaze.
Stair, a step.
Stake, a post.
Steak, a piece of flesh.
Steel, hardened iron.
Steal, to take by theft.
Stile, steps into a field.
Style, manner of writing.
Strait, narrow.
Straight, not crooked.
Suck' er, a young shoot.
Suc' cour, aid, help.
Sum, the whole.
Some, a part.
Sun, cause of day.
Son, a male child.
Sut' tle, neat weight.
Subt' le, artful.
Tale, a story.
Tail, the end.
Tare, weight allowed.
Tear, to rend.
Tax, a rate.
Tacks, small nails.
Teem, to produce.
Team, horses or oxen drawing a carriage.

10*

Terse, smooth, neat.
Tierce, a liquid measure
The, the article.
Thee, thyself.
There, in that place.
Their, of them.
Threw, did throw.
Through, from end to end.
Throw, to fling.
Throe, agony.
Throne, seat of a king.
Thrown, flung, cast.
Time, measure of duration.
Thyme, a plant.
Tier, (*teer*,) a row, a rank.
Tear, water from the eyes.
Too, likewise.
To, unto.
Two, twice one.
Tow, refuse of flax, to draw by a rope.
Toe, part of the foot.
Tole, to draw by degrees.
Toll, a tax.
Tongue, (*tung*) organ of speech.
Tong, catch of a buckle.
Tray, a utensil.
Trey, three at cards or dice.
Tun, a large cask.
Ton, 20 hundred weight.

Vale, a valley.
Vail, ⎰ a covering for
Veil, ⎱ the face.
Vane, a weathercock.
Vain, meanly proud.
Vein, a blood vessel.
Waste, loss.
Waist, part of the body.
Wale, rising part in cloth.
Wail, to sorrow.
Wait, to tarry.
Weight, heaviness.
Ware, merchandise.
Wear, to put on, a dam to catch fish in.
Way, a road.
Weigh, to poise.
Week, seven days.
Weak, not strong.
Week'ly, every week.
Weak'ly, feebly.
Ween, to think.
Wean, to withdraw from any habit.
Weth'er, a male sheep.
Weath'er, state of the air.
Wood, trees.
Would, was willing.
Ye, *plural of* thou.
Yea, yes.
You, *plural of* thou.
Yew, a tree.
Ewe, a female sheep.

CHAPTER XXV.

Words often improperly confounded in spelling or pronunciation.

Ac cept', to take.
Ex cept', to leave out.
Ap praise', to set a price on.
Ap prize', to inform.
Cel' e ry, a species of parsley.
Sal' a ry, stated hire.
Chron' i cal, of long duration.
Chron' i cle, a history.
Coun' cil, an assembly.
Coun' sel, advice.
Cur' rant, a fruit.
Cur' rent, a stream.
Cur'ri er, a leather dresser.
Côu rier', a messenger.
Cym' bal, a musical instrument.
Sym' bol, a type.
Er' rand, a message.
Er' rant, wandering.
Ar' rant, vile, wicked.
Ex' tant, now in being.
Ex tent', compass of a thing.
Fran' cis, a man's name.
Fran'ces, a woman's name.

Ge'ni us, mental power.
Ge' nus, a class of be- ings.
In ge' ni ous, inventive.
In gen' u ous, open, can- did.
Ker' nel, the seed of fruit.
Colo' nel, a military officer.
Lay, to place, to quiet.
Lie, to rest, to recline on a bed.
Lick' er ish, delicate.
Lic' o rice, a sweet root.
Prac' tice, use, habit.
Prac' tise, to use, to do habitually.
Prin' ci ple, first rule.
Prin' ci pal, chief.
Proph' e cy, a prediction.
Proph' e sy,* to predict.
Tract, a quantity of land, a small book.
Track, a mark left.
Val' ue, worth, price.
Val' ley, a vale

* y like i long.

CHAPTER XXVI.

Words which agree in orthography, but differ in accent, pronunciation, or meaning.

Ab' stract, an abridgment.

Ab stract', to draw from.

  A buse', ill treatment.

  A buse', to treat rudely.

Ac' cent, force of voice.

Ac cent,' to place the ac-
  -cent.

  At' tri bute, a quality.

  At trib' ute, to ascribe.

Au' gust, the name of a
  month.

Au gust', magnificent.

  Cem' ent, what joins
  bodies together.

  Ce ment', to unite.

Close, compact.

Close, to unite.

  Com' pact, an agree-
  ment.

  Com pact', close, firm.

Com' pound, a mixture.

Com pound', to mingle.

  Con' cert, harmony.

  Con cert', to contrive.

Con' duct, management.

Con duct', to manage.

  Con' jure, to practise
  enchantment.

  Con jure', to enjoin
  solemnly.

Con' test, a dispute.

Con test', to contend.

  Con' tract, an agree-
  ment.

  Con tract', to bargain.

Con' trast, opposition.

Con trast', to place in opposition.

  Con' vert, a person
  verted.

  Con vert', to change.

Con' vict, a person con-
  victed.

Con vict', to prove guilty.

  Cour' te sy, civility,
  respect.

  Courte'sy, act of respect
  made by a woman.

Cruise, a small cup.

Cruise, to sail.

Des' ert, a wilderness.

De sert', to forsake.

Des' sert, the last course
  of an entertainment.

Dis' count, an allowance.

Dis count', to deduct.

  En' trance, admission.

  En trance', to put into
  ecstasy.

Es' cort, a convoy.

Es cort', to guard.

Ex cuse', an apology.

Ex cuse', to accept an apology.

Ex'port, a thing exported.

Ex port', to send abroad.

Ex' tract, a quotation.

Ex tract', to draw out of.

Fer' ment, inward motion.

Fer ment', to have inward motion. [curring.

Fre' quent, often oc-

Fre quent', to visit often

Gal' lant, brave.

Gal lant', a beau.

Grease, fat.

Grease, to smear with fat

House, a place of abode.

House, to shelter. [ed.

Im'port, a thing import-

Im port', to bring from abroad.

In' crease, augmentation.

In crease', to make more.

In' sult, an affront.

In sult', to affront.

In văl' id, of no force.

In va lid', (*in va leed'*,) a disabled person.

Let, to lease, to permit.

Let, to. hinder.

Min' ute, sixty seconds.

Mi nute', small. [head.

Mouth, aperture in the

Mouth, to chew.

Ob'ject, that on which we are employed.

Ob ject', to oppose.

O'ver throw, destruction.

O ver throw', to destroy.

Pres' ent, a gift.

Pre sent', to give.

Prod' uce, product, a-mount. [effect.

Pro duce', to cause, to

Proj' ect, a scheme.

Pro ject', to contrive.

Reb'el, one who rebels.

Re bel', to oppose.

Rec' ord, a register.

Re cord', to register.

Ref' use, the worthless part.

Re fuse', to reject.

Rise, the act of rising.

Rise, to move upwards.

Sub'ject, matter treated of; one under the do-minion of another.

Sub ject', to enslave.

Tor' ment, pain, anguish.

Tor ment', to put in pain.

Trans' port, rapture.

Trans port', to put in an ecstasy.

Use, the act of employing.

Use, to employ.

*W*reath, a garland

*W*reath, to interweave.

A MORNING IN SPRING.

Lo ! the bright, the rosy morning
   Calls me forth to take the air ;
Cheerful spring, with smiles returning,
   Ushers in the new-born year.

Nature, now in all her beauty,
   With her gently-moving tongue,
Prompts me to the pleasing duty,
   Of a grateful morning song.

See the early blossoms springing !
   See the jocund lambkins play !
Hear the lark and linnet singing,
   Welcome to the new-born day !

Vernal music, softly sounding,
   Echoes through the verdant grove :
Nature now, with life abounding,
   Swells with harmony and love.

Now the kind refreshing showers,
   Water all the plains around ;
Springing grass, and painted flowers,
   In the smiling meads abound.

Now their vernal dress assuming,
   Leafy robes adorn the trees ;
Odours now, the air perfuming,
   Sweetly swell the gentle breeze,

Praise to thee, thou great Creator !
   Praise be thine from ev'ry tongue ;
Join, my soul, with every creature ;
   Join the universal song.

For ten thousand bless;ngs giv'n ;
   For the richest gifts bestow'd ;
Sound his praise through earth and heav'n,
   Sound Jehovah's praise aloud !

HEAVENLY WISDOM.

How happy is the man who hears
   Instruction's warning voice,
And who celestial Wisdom makes
   His early, only choice.

For she has treasures greater far
   Than east or west unfold ;
And her reward is more secure
   Than is the gain of gold.

In her right hand she holds to view
   A length of happy years ;
And in her left, the prize of fame
   And honour bright appears.

She guides the young with innocence,
   In pleasure's path to tread ;
A crown of glory she bestows
   Upon the hoary head.

According as her labours rise,
 So her rewards increase ;
Her ways are ways of pleasantness,
 And all her paths are peace.

ON EARLY RISING.

How foolish they who lengthen night,
And slumber in the morning light !
How sweet at early morning's rise,
To view the glories of the skies,
And mark with curious eye the sun
Prepare his radiant course to run !
Its fairest form then nature wears,
And clad in brightest green appears.
The sprightly lark, with artless lay,
Proclaims the entrance of the day.
How sweet to breathe the gale's perfume,
And feast the eye with nature's bloom !
Along the dewy lawn to rove,
And hear the music of the grove !
Nor you, ye delicate and fair,
Neglect to taste the morning air ;
This will your nerves with vigour brace ;
Improve and heighten every grace ;
Add to your breath a rich perfume ;
And to your cheeks a fairer bloom ;
With lustre teach your eyes to glow ;
And health and cheerfulness bestow.

CRUELTY TO INSECTS CONDEMNED.

A certain youth indulged himself in the cruel entertainment of torturing and killing flies. He tore off their wings and legs, and then watched with pleasure their feeble efforts to escape him. Sometimes he collected a number of them together, and crushed them at once to death ; glorying, like many a celebrated hero, in the devastation he committed. His tutor remonstrated with him in vain on this barbarous conduct. He could not persuade him to believe that flies are capable of pain, and have a right, no less than ourselves, to life, liberty, and enjoyment. The signs of agony, which, when tormented, they express, by the quick and various contortions of their bodies, he neither understood nor regarded.

The tutor had a microscope ; and he desired his pupil, one day, to examine a most beautiful and surprising animal. " Observe," said he, " how it is studded from head to tail with black and silver, and its body all over beset with the most curious bristles !" The head contains the most lively eyes, encircled with silver hairs ; and the trunk consists of two parts, folded over each other. The whole body is ornamented with plumes and decorations, which surpass all the luxuries of dress, in the courts of the greatest princes." Pleased and astonished with what he saw,

11

the youth was impatient to know the name
and properties of the wonderful animal. It
was withdrawn from the magnifier; and when
offered to his naked eye, proved to be a poor
fly, which had been the victim of his wanton
cruelty.

HEALTH.

Who is she that with graceful steps, and
with lively air, trips over yonder plain ?

The rose blushes on her cheeks; the
sweetness of the morning breathes from her
lips; joy tempered with innocence and modesty, sparkles in her eyes ; and the cheerfulness of her heart appears in all her move-
ments. Her name is Health: she is the
daughter of Exercise and Temperance.
Their sons inhabit the mountain and the
plain. They are brave, active, and lovely,
and partake of all the beauties and virtues
of their sister. Vigour strings their nerves,
strength dwells in their bones, and labour is
their delight all the day long. The employ-
ments of their father excite their appetites ;
and the repasts of their mother refresh them.
To combat the passions, is their delight ; to
conquer evil habits, their glory. Their
pleasures are moderate ; and therefore they
endure ; their repose is short, but sound and
undisturbed. Their blood is pure ; their
minds are serene ; and the physician does
not find the way to their habitations.

CHARITY.

Happy is the man who has sown in his breast the seeds of charity and love! From the fountain of his heart rise rivers of goodness; and the streams overflow for the benefit of mankind. He assists the poor in their trouble! he rejoices in promoting the welfare of all men. He does not harshly censure his neighbour; he believes not the tales of envy and malevolence, nor repeats their slanders. He forgives the injuries of men; he wipes them from his remembrance: revenge and malice have no place in his heart. For evil he returns not evil: he hates not even his enemies, but requites their injustice with friendly admonition. The griefs and anxieties of men excite his compassion; he endeavours to alleviate the weight of their misfortunes; and the pleasure of success re-

wards his labour. He calms the fury, he
heals the quarrels of angry men ; and pre-
vents the mischiefs of strife and animosity.
He promotes in his neighbourhood peace
and good will ; and his name is repeated
with praiseand benedictions.

ON ANGER.

Before you give way to anger, try to find a
reason for not being angry. To be angry is
to punish yourself for the faults of others.
If a word, dropped by chance from your
friend, give you offence, avoid a hasty reply,
and beware of telling the cause of your anger to those persons whom you meet. When
you are cool, it will vanish, and leave no traces behind it. Wrath kindles wrath ; make
it a constant rule, therefore, never to speak
a single word while you are angry.

Never indulge revenge to your own hurt.
The sharpest revenge is to despise the affront ; it will then return on him who has giv-
en the offence, and torment him with the
sting of remorse. If those who hate you
can put you to pain, it will give them fresh
vigour : on this account, do not expose your
weak side to them, nor show them whither
to direct a second blow.

TO A BOY;

On confining a Bird in a Cage.

RICHARD, what greater punishment
  Could I inflict, my boy, on thee;
And tell me what would grieve thee more,
  Than thus to lose thy liberty.

Yet thou canst take a savage joy
  To view thy captive's fond desires;
Thou canst with unrelenting heart,
  Behold him beat against the wires.

See, he extends his fluttering wings,
  His bloody beak, does now implore.
He prays thee in the softest notes
  To let him go, nor pain him more.

Confinement thou could'st never bear
  With patience for a single hour;
How canst thou then, unthinking boy,
  Thus torture those within thy power?

Remember, that corporeal pain
  Each bird, each animal can feel;
Though power of language is denied
  Their suffering torments to reveal.

So now, my child, attend my prayer,
  And set thy fluttering captive free;
That if thou e'er shouldst be confined,
  I may restore thy liberty.

11*

GOD IS OUR FATHER.

The mother loves her little child; she brings it up in her arms; she nourishes its body with food; she feeds its mind with knowledge; if it is sick, she nurses it with tender love; she watches over it when it is asleep; she forgets it not for a moment; she rejoices daily in its growth.

But who is the parent of the mother? Who nourishes her with good things, and watches over her with tender love, and remembers her every moment? Whose arms are about her to guard her from harm? And if she is sick, who shall heal her?

God is the parent of the mother; He is the parent of all, for He *created* all. All the men and all the women, who are alive in the wide world, are His children; He loveth all and is good to all.

PROVIDENCE.

" I have been thrown from my pony," said a little boy to his father : " but by *chance* I am not hurt." " I am glad to hear of your safe escape, my dear child, but you ought to ascribe it to PROVIDENCE. *Chance* is blind, and cannot protect us; PROVIDENCE watches over all."

" Look round on Nature—on those things most obvious to your senses—on plants, trees, animals, and even yourself: lift your eyes to Heaven—see the beautiful regularity of the planetary orbs, the return of day and night, and the revolution of seasons; then reflect—can these things be the effect of Chance? No! A Supreme Power rules and directs the order of the universe, and holds the chain of events. Learn to acknowledge this great and good Being in every thing that befals you. Pay him the homage of grateful praise for his benefits; adore his unsearchable wisdom when he afflicts; and repose a humble confidence in his mercy and protection, amidst the various ills that beset the path of human life. Extend your views beyond the present scene to permanent possessions and pure pleasures; and entitle yourself to their enjoyment, by studying to obey the will of Him who placed you here. Look up to his superintending Providence for every blessing you would wish to receive, and for security from every danger you are anxious to avoid; and scorn to be indebted to *Chance* for what you really owe to your FATHER and your GOD."

CHAPTER XXVII.

Of the Letters.

" Orthography teaches the nature and powers of letters, and the just method of spelling words.

A letter is the first principle, or least part of a word.

The letters of the English language, called the English Alphabet, are twenty-six in number.

The letters are the representatives of certain articulate sounds, the elements of the language. An articulate sound, is the sound of the human voice formed by the organs of speech.

Letters are divided into vowels and consonants.

A vowel is an articulate sound, that can be perfectly uttered by itself: as, *a, e, o;* which are formed without the help of any other sound.

A consonant is an articulate sound, which cannot be perfectly uttered without the help of a vowel; as, *b, d, f, l;* which require vowels to express them fully.

The vowels are, *a, e, i, o, u,* and sometimes *w,* and *y.*

W and *y* are consonants when they begin a word or syllable: but in every other situation they are vowels.

The consonants are divided into mutes and semi-vowels.

The mutes cannot be sounded *at all* without the aid of a vowel. They are *b, p, t, d, k,* and *c* and *g* hard.

The semi-vowels have an imperfect sound of themselves. They are, *f, l, m, n, r, v, s, x, z,* and *c,* and *g* soft.

⁄ Four of the semi-vowels, namely, *l, m, n, r*, are also distinguished by the name of *liquids*, from their readily uniting with other consonants, and flowing as it were into their sounds."

CHAPTER XXVIII.
Sounds of the Consonants.

B.

B has one sound: as in *baker*. When followed by *t* or preceded by *m* in the same syllable it is generally silent: as in *debt, plumb*.

C.

C has two regular sounds, hard and soft: hard like *k*, before *a, o, u, l*, and *r ;* as in *card, cord, curd, clay, crawl :* soft like *s* before *e, i,* and *y ;* as in *cedar, city, cymbal.* Besides these, it sounds like *z* in a few words; as *sacrifice, discern*. And when followed by *i* and *e* before a vowel, it slides into the sound of *sh ;* as in *ocean, social*.

CH.

CH have three sounds: 1st. like *tch*, as in *cheese ;* 2d. like *k*, as in *chord ;* 3d. like *sh*, as in *chaise*.

D.

D has two sounds: its proper sound, as in *dress, bold ;* and the sound of *j*, as in *soldier*. The verbal termination *ed*, when not preceded by *d* or *t*, is generally sounded like *t ;* as *stuffed, hissed*, pronounced *stuft, hist ;* except in solemn style, and in some cases where the word is an adjective, as " a *learned* man."

F.

F has one sound, as in *life, fever ;* except in *of*, where it has the sound of *v*. It is never silent.

G.

G has two sounds, hard and soft : hard as in *game, gone ;* soft, as in *gem, giant.* It always sounds hard before *a, o, u, l,* and *r ;* and is sometimes hard, and sometimes soft, before *e, i,* and *y.* It is silent before *n,* in the same syllable.

GH.

GH are sounded like *f,* as in *laugh, cough ;* or are silent, as in *bough, plough.*

H

H has one sound, as in *hat, horse.*

J.

J has one sound, that of soft *g ;* as in *joy.* Except *hallelujah,* where it sounds like *y.* It is never silent.

K.

K has one sound, as in *king.* It is silent before *n,* as in *knife.*

L.

L has one sound, as in *love, billow.* It is doubled at the end of monosyllables.

M.

M has one sound as in *murmur ;* and is never silent.

N.

N has one sound as in *name.* When it ends a syllable preceded by *m* it is silent.

P.

P has one sound, as in *pond.*

PH.

PH sounds like *f,* as in *phantom ;* or ars silent, as in *phthisic ;* except in *Stephen,* where they sound like *v.*

Q.

Q is always followed by *u :* they sound like *k,* as in *antique, liquor ;* or like *kw,* as in *question, quadrant ;* and are never silent.

R.

R has one sound, as in *river, rage ;* and is never silent.

S.

S has two regular sounds, hard or sharp, and soft or flat : sharp, as in *sister, sun ;* soft, as in *was, rose.* It also sometimes sounds like *sh ;* as in *sugar, dimension ;* and like *zh :* as in *pleasure, evasion.*

T.

T has three sounds : 1st. its proper sound, as in *tattle ;* 2d. when followed by *u* with the accent on the syllable immediately preceding, it sounds like *tch :* as in *nature, virtue ;* 3d. when followed by *i* before another vowel it sounds like *sh :* as in *nation, portion ;* except when preceded by *s,* or *x,* in which case it sounds like *tch :* as in *christian, mixtion.*

V.

V has one sound, as in *value.* It is silent in *sevennight* only.

W.

W, when a consonant, has nearly the sound of *oo,* as in *watr.*

X.

X has two regular sounds, sharp and flat : sharp like *ks,* as in *exercise, excellent ;* flat like *gz,* as in *example, examine.* It also sounds like *z* at the beginning of words ; as in *Xerxes ;* and is never silent.

Y, when a consonant, has nearly the sound of *ee,* as in *youth.*

Z.

Z has one sound : as in *zone, bronze.*

~~~~~~~~~~~~

CHAPTER XXIX.

Diphthongs and Triphthongs.

" A diphthong is the union of two vowels, pronounced by a single impulse of the voice : as *ea* in *beat, ou* in *sound.*

A proper diphthong is that in which both the vowels are sounded : as, *oi* in *voice, ou* in *ounce.*

An improper diphthong has but one of the vowels sounded : as, *ea* in *eagle, oa* in *boat.*

A triphthong is the union of three vowels, pronounced by a single impulse of the voice : as *eau,* in *beau, iew* in *view.*

SYLLABLES.

A syllable is a sound, either simple or compound pronounced by a single impulse of the voice, and constituting a word, or a part of a word : as *a, an, ant.*

Spelling is the art of rightly dividing words into their syllables, or of expressing a word by its proper letters.

WORDS.

Words are articulate sounds, used by common consent, as signs of our ideas.

A word of one syllable is termed a Monosyllable ; a word of two syllables, a Dissyllable ; a word of three syllables, a Trisyllable; a word of four or more syllables, a Polysyllable."

All words are either primitive, derivative, or compound.

" A primitive word is one which cannot be reduced to any simpler word in the language : as *man, good, content.*

A derivative word is one which may be reduced to another word in English of greater simplicity : as *manful, goodness, contentment.*"

A compound word is formed of two or more words : as *penknife, teacup, Yorkshire.*

~~~~~~~~~

CHAPTER XXX.

Rules for Spelling.

" Rule 1. Monosyllables ending with *f, l,* or *s,* preceded by a single vowel, double the final consonant : as, *staff, mill, pass.* The only exceptions are, *of, if, as, is, has, gas, was, pus, yes, his, this, us* and *thus.*

Rule 2. Monosyllables ending with any consonant but *f, l,* or *s,* and preceded by a single vowel, seldom double the final consonant. Exceptions : *add, ebb, butt, egg, odd, err, inn, bunn, burr, purr,* and *buzz.*

Rule 3. Words ending with *y,* preceded by a consonant, form the plurals of nouns, the persons of verbs, verbal nouns, past participles, comparatives and superlatives, by changing *y* into *i* : as, *spy,*

12

spies; I *carry,* thou *carriest,* he *carries; carrier, carried; happy, happier, happiest.*

The present participle in *ing,* retains the *y,* that *i* may not be doubled; as, *carry, carrying; bury, burying.*

But *y,* preceded by a vowel, in such instances as the above, is not changed; as, *boy, boys; cloy, cloyed;* except in *lay, pay, say,* from which are formed, *laid, paid, said.*

Rule 4. Words ending with *y,* preceded by a consonant, upon assuming an additional syllable beginning with a consonant, commonly change *y* into *i;* as, *happy, happily, happiness.* But when *y* is preceded by a vowel, it is very rarely changed: as, *boy, boyish, boyhood; joy, joyless, joyful.*

Rule 5. Monosyllables, and words accented on the last syllable, ending with a single consonant, preceded by a single vowel, double that consonant, when they take another syllable beginning with a vowel: as, *wit, witty; thin, thinnish; begin, beginner, beginning.*

But if a diphthong precedes, or the accent is on the preceding syllable, the consonant remains single: as, *toil, toiling; offer, offering; maid, maiden.*

Rule 6.—Words ending with any double letter but *l,* and taking *ness, less, ly,* or *ful,* after them, preserve the letter double; as, *harmlessness, carelessness, carelessly, stiffly, successful, distressful.* But those words which end with double *l,* and take *ness, less, ly,* or *ful* after them, generally omit one *l:* as, *fulness, skilless, fully, skilful.*

Rule 7. *Ness, less, ly,* and *ful,* added to words ending with silent *e,* do not cut it off; as, *paleness, guileness, closely, peaceful ;* except in a few words; as, *duly, truly, awful.*

Rule 8. *Ment,* joined to words ending with silent *e,* generally preserves the *e* from elision : as, *abatement, chastisement, incitement.* The words *judgment, abridgment, acknowledgment,* are devia-tions from the rule.

Like other terminations, *ment* canges *y* into *i,* when preceded by a consonant ; as, *accompany, accompaniment ; merry, merriment.*

Rule 9. *Able* and *ible,* when incorporated into words ending with silent *e,* usually cut it off : as, *blame, blamable ; cure, curable ; sense, sensible.* But if *c,* or *g* soft comes before *e* in the original word, the *e* is preserved : as, *change, changeable ; peace, peaceable.*

Rule 10. When *ing* or *ish* is added to words ending with silent *e,* the *e* is usually omitted : as, *place, placing ; lodge, lodging ; slave, slavish.*

CHAPTER XXXI.

Accent.

" Accent is the laying of a peculiar stress of voice, on a certain letter or syllable of a word, that it may be better heard than the rest, or distin-guished from them : as in the word *presume,* the stress of voice must be on the letter *u,* and second syllable *sume.*"

Emphasis.

Emphasis is a strong and full sound of voice, by which we distinguish some word or words on which we design to lay particular stress, in order to convey the true meaning of the sentence.

Inflections of the Voice.

" The inflection of the voice is that *upward*, or *downward* slide, which the voice makes when the pronunciation of a word is finishing; and which may therefore not improperly be called the *rising*, and the *falling* inflection."

The rising inflection is that modulation of the voice, usually called an elevation, and sometimes the suspending pause ; and which is to be heard in a correct pronunciation of the final syllable of the word *earnest* in the following example: " Are you in earnest ?"

The falling inflection is that modulation of the voice called a depression, a cadence, or closing pause ; and is to be heard in pronouncing the final word of this example: " I am in earnest."

CHAPTER XXXII.

Punctuation.

Punctuation is the art of dividing a written composition into sentences, and parts of sentences, by points or stops, for the purpose of marking the different pauses, and, in some measure, pointing out the inflections of the voice, which the sense, and an accurate pronunciation require.

The principal points are,

The Comma	,
The Semicolon	;
The Colon	:
The Period	.
The Interrogation point	?
The Exclamation point	!
The Parenthesis	()
The Dash	—

The Comma is a pause in reading until you may count one ;* and usually requires the rising inflection of the voice.

The Semicolon is a pause until you may count two ; and should have sometimes the rising, and sometimes the falling inflection, as the sense or harmony requires. If the sense be perfect, the falling inflection should generally be adopted ; if imperfect, the rising.

The Colon is a pause until you may count three; and requires the falling inflection of the voice, except in comparative sentences.

The Period is a pause until you may count four; and commonly requires the falling inflection.

---

* The quantity or duration of each pause cannot be exactly defined. Grave and solemn compositions, and those containing long periods, require longer pauses than those which are written in familiar language, or broken into short periods. Persons who are reading to a large auditory must make longer pauses than when a few persons only are in hearing. And a judicious reader will frequently make pauses in reading, where none are marked in printing. Although no precise rules can be given for the length of the pauses, yet the practice of defining the duration with numeral adjectives is sufficiently exact for common use.

12*

The Interrogation Point shows that a question is asked : as, " What do you see?"   It usually requires a pause long enough to count four ; and the rising inflection of the voice, unless the question be asked with an interrogative word; such as, *who, which, what, when, how, where;* in this case it requires the falling inflection.

The Exclamation Point is used to denote some passion or emotion ; as, wonder, surprise, admiration, &c.   The length of the pause, and the inflection of the voice, must be governed by the sense.

The Parenthesis includes a part of a sentence, which may be omitted without injuring the sense, and must be read in a quicker and lower tone than the rest.   The pause and inflection of voice at the end of the parenthesis, should be the same as are required by the word immediately preceding it.

The Dash, when used alone, denotes a sudden pause, or unexpected change in the subject, and is to be treated much like a comma ; where used with any other point it lengthens the pause.

Besides these, there are other characters used in writing, viz.

An Accent (') shows the stress of voice in pronouncing a word to be on that syllable, over or immediately after which it is placed.   Some writers make use of two accents, the grave (') and the acute (').   The grave is applied to long syllables; the acute, to short.

The grave accent is also used to denote the middle or grave sound of the vowel *a.*

The acute accent is also used to denote the irregular sounds of *a, e, i,* and *o,* which correspond with short *u.*

A Breve (ˇ) shows that the vowel over which it is placed sounds short.

A Hyphen (-) is used to connect compound words, and parts of words at the ends of lines. The same mark placed over a vowel, denotes that it sounds long.

A Circumflex (ˆ) placed over a vowel, denotes the broad sound of *a*, and the middle sound of *o*, and *u*.

A Diæresis (¨) is placed over the last of two vowels, that would otherwise make a diphthong, and parts them into two syllables; as, Raphaël, Creätor.

Brackets, [], and sometimes the Parenthesis, are used to include words that explain a foregoing word or sentence.

A Quotation (" ") includes a passage, transcribed from another author. The passage has two inverted commas at the beginning, and two direct ones at the end of it.

An Apostrophe (') is the sign of the possessive case; and likewise denotes the omission of a letter: as, John's book; lov'd for loved.

A Caret (ʌ) shows where to bring in what was omitted through mistake. It is never used in printing.

An Ellipsis (———*or* - - - -) shows that some letter in a word, or some words in a sentence, are intentionally omitted; as, k—g for king.

An Index or Hand (☞) points to something that requires particular attention.

A Paragraph (¶) denotes the beginning of a new subject; it is chiefly used in the Bible.

A Section (§) is used to divide a chapter into less parts.

A Brace } is used to connect several lines with one common term; and in poetry it is used at the end of a triplet of three lines.

An Asterisk (*), Obelisk (†), Double Obelisk (‡), Parallels (||), Section (§), and letters and figures, are used as references to notes at the bottom of the page.

~~~~~~~~~~~~

CHAPTER XXXIII.

Capitals.

The following words should begin with capitals:

1. The first word of every book, chapter, letter, note, bill, receipt, or any other piece of writing.

2. The first word after a period; and, if two sentences are totally independent, after the interrogation or exclamation.

3. The names and titles of the Deity.

4. Names of persons, places, ships, rivers, mountains, titles, professions, &c.

5. Adjectives derived from the names of places; as, English, Spanish.

6. The first word of every line in poetry.

7. The principal word in the titles of books.

8. The pronoun I, and the interjection O.

9. Words of particular importance; as, the Revolution, the Reformation.

10. The names of the months, and the days of the week: as January, February, Sunday, Monday.

CHAPTER XXXIV.

Abbreviations used in Writing and Printing.

A. *or* ans. Answer.

A. A. S. Fellow of the American Academy of Arts and Sciences.

A. B. *or* B. A. Bachelor of Arts.

Abp. Archbishop.

Acct. Account.

A. D. In the year of our Lord,

Admr. Administrator.

A. M. *or* M. A. Master of Arts.

A. M. In the year of the World. Before noon.

Apr. April.

Aug. August.

Bar. *or* bbl. Barrel.

Bart. Baronet.

Benj. Benjamin.

B. C. Before Christ.

B. D. Bachelor of Divinity.

Bp. Bishop.

B. V. Blessed Virgin.

Capt. Captain.

C. *or* cent. a hundred.

Cant. Canticles.

C. C. County Court.

C. C. P. Court of Common Pleas.

Ch. *or* Chap. Chapter.

Chron. Chronicles.

Co. Company. County.

Col. Colonel. Colossians.

Com. Commodore.

Comr. Commissioner.

Con. Connecticut.

Cor. Corinthians.

Cr. Credit.

C. S. Court of Sessions.

Cwt. Hundred weight.

Dan. Daniel.

d. a penny.

D. D. Doctor of Divinity.

Dec. December.

Del. Delaware.

Dep. Deputy

Deut. Deuteronomy.

Do. *or* Ditto. The same.

Dolls. *or* $. Dollars.

Doz. Dozen.

Doct. *or* Dr. Doctor.

Dr. Doctor. Debtor.

dr. Drams.

Dwt. *or* dwt. Pennyweight.

E. East.

Eben. Ebenezer.

Eccl. Ecclesiastes.

Ecclus. Ecclesiasticus.

Ed. Edition. Editor.

E. g. *or* e. g. For example.

Ep. Epistle.

Eph. Ephesians.

Eng. English. England.

Esq. Esquire.

Ex. Example. Exodus

Exr. Executor.

F. A. S. Fellow of the Antiquarian Society.

F. R. S. Fellow of the Royal Society.

Feb. February.

Fol. Folio.

Fur. Furlong.

Gal.	Galatians; Gallon.	Mo.	Month.
Geo.	George. Georgia.	Mr.	Master. (*pron. Mister.*)
Gen.	Genesis. General.	Mrs.	Mistress. (,, *Missis.*)
Gent.	Gentleman.	MS.	Manuscript.
Gov.	Governour.	MSS.	Manuscripts.
G. R.	George the King.	N.	Note. North.
grs.	grains.	Nath.	Nathaniel.
Heb.	Hebrews.	N. B.	Take Notice.
Hhd.	Hogshead.		New Brunswick.
Hon.	Honourable.	N. C.	North Carolina.
hund.	hundred.	N. L.	New England.
Ib. *or* Ibid. *or* Ibidem. In			North East.
the same place,		N. H.	New Hampshire.
Id. *or* Idem. The same.		N. J.	New Jersey.
i. e.	that is.	No.	Number.
Isa.	Isaiah.	Nov.	November.
Jan.	January.	N. S.	New Style.
Jer.	Jeremiah.		Nova Scotia.
Jno.	John.	N. T.	New Testament.
Jona.	Jonathan.	N. W.	Northwest.
Jos.	Joseph.	Num.	Numbers.
Josh.	Joshua.	N. Y.	New York.
Jun. *or* Jr. Junior.		Obj.	Objection.
Jus. Pac. Justice of the		Obt.	Obedient.
Peace.		Oct.	October.
K.	King.	O. S.	Old Style.
Ken. *or* Ky. Kentucky.		Oz.	Ounce.
Km.	Kingdom.	p.	page.
Knt. *or* Kt. Knight.		pp.	pages.
Lev.	Leviticus.	Per cent.	By the hundred.
Lib.	a book.	Penn. *or* Pa. Pennsylvania.	
£.	a pound *in money.*	P. M.	Afternoon.
lb.	a pound *in weight.*		Post Master.
Lieut. *or* Lt. Lieutenant.		P.M.G.	PostMaster General.
LL. D. Doctor of Laws.		Prof.	Professor.
L. S. Place of the Seal.		Pres.	President.
Maj.	Major.	P. S.	Postscript.
Mar.	March.	Ps.	Psalm.
Mass. *or* Ms. Massachusetts.		Q.	Question. Queen.
Matt.	Matthew.	q.	farthing.
M. B.	Bachelor of Physic.	q. d.	as if he should say.
M. D.	Doctor of Physic.	q. l.	as much as you please.
Md.	Maryland.	q. s.	a sufficient quantity.
Me.	Maine.	qr.	quarter of a Cwt.
Messrs. Gentlemen. Sirs.		qt.	quart.

Rev. Revelation. Reverend.
Regr. Register.
R. I. Rhode Island.
Robt. Robert.
Rt. Hon. Right Honourable.
Rt. Rev. Right Reverend.
S. *or* s. shilling.
S. South.
St. Saint.
Sam. Samuel.
Sept. September.
Servt. Servant.
S. C. South Carolina.
    Supreme Court.
    Superior Court.
S. E. Southeast.
S. H. S. Fellow of the Historical Society.
S. T. D. Doctor of Divinity.
S. T. P. Professor of Divinity
ſs. To wit. Namely.
S. W. Southwest.
S. J. C. Supreme Judicial Court.
T. Ton.
Ten. Tennessee.
Theo. Theophilus.
Thess. Thessalonians.

Tho. Thomas.
U. C. Year of Rome.
Ult. The last.
U. S. United States.
U. S. A. United States of America.
v. *or* ver. verse.
v. *or* vide. See.
Vir. *or* Va. Virginia.
Viz. To wit. Namely.
Vol. Volume.
Vols. Volumes.
Ver. *or* Vt. Vermont.
W. West.
W. I. West India. West Indies.
Wm. William.
Yd. Yard.
Yds. Yards.
&. and.
&c. and so forth.
4to. quarto.
8vo. Octavo.
12mo. Duodecimo.
1st. first.
2d. second.
3d. third.
4th. fourth.

Names of the Months, with the number of Days.

January	31		July	31
February	28		August	31
March	31		September	30
April	30		October	31
May	31		November	30
June	30		December	31

CHAPTER XXXV.

Figures and Numbers.

Figures.	Numbers.	Names.	Numerical Adjectives.
1	I	One	first
2	II	Two	second
3	III	Three	third
4	IV	Four	fourth
5	V	Five	fifth
6	VI	Six	sixth
7	VII	Seven	seventh
8	VIII	Eight	eighth
9	IX	Nine	ninth
10	X	Ten	tenth
11	XI	Eleven	eleventh
12	XII	Twelve	twelfth
13	XIII	Thirteen	thirteenth
14	XIV	Fourteen	fourteenth
15	XV	Fifteen	fifteenth
16	XVI	Sixteen	sixteenth
17	XVII	Seventeen	seventeenth
18	XVIII	Eighteen	eighteenth
19	XIX	Nineteen	nineteenth
20	XX	Twenty	twentieth
30	XXX	Thirty	thirtieth
40	XL	Forty	fortieth
50	L	Fifty	fiftieth
60	LX	Sixty	sixtieth
70	LXX	Seventy	seventieth
80	LXXX	Eighty	eightieth
90	XC	Ninety	ninetieth
100	C	One hundred	one hundredth
200	CC	Two hundred	two hundredth
300	CCC	Three hundred	three hundredth
400	CCCC	Four hundred	four hundredth
500	D	Five hundred	five hundredth
600	DC	Six hundred	six hundredth
700	DCC	Seven hundred	seven hundredth
800	DCCC	Eight hundred	eight hundredth
900	DCCCC	Nine hundred	nine hundredth
1000	M	One thousand	one thousandth

Questions for Examination.

ON CHAPTER 1.

What are the sounds of *a* ?
    ,,   ,,   of *e* ?
    ,,   ,,   of *i* ?
    ,,   ,,   of *o* ?
    ,,   ,,   of *u* ?

What irregular sounds has *a* ?
    ,,   ,,   has *e* ?
    ,,   ,,   has *i* ?
    ,,   ,,   has *o* ?
    ,,   ,,   has *y* ?

What are the combined sounds of *oi* and *oy* ?
    ,,   ,,   ,,   of *ou* and *ow* ?
What sound has the diphthong *ai* ?
What sounds has   ,,   *au* ?
What sound has   ,,   *aw* ?
What sound has   ,,   *ay* ?
What sounds has   ,,   *ea* ?
What sound has   ,,   *ee* ?
What sounds has   ,,   *ei* ?
What sound has   ,,   *ew* ?
What sounds has   ,,   *ie* ?
What sound has   ,,   *oa* ?
What sound has   ,,   *oe* ?
What sounds has   ,,   *oo* ?

What are the sounds of *c* ?
    ,,   ,,   of *ch* ?
    ,,   ,,   of *d* ?
    ,,   ,,   of *g* ?
What is the sound of *gh* ?
    ,,   ,,   of *ph* ?
What are the sounds of *s* ?
    ,,   ,,   of *t* ?
    ,,   ,,   of *th* ?
    ,,   ,,   of *x* ?

ON CHAPTER 27.

What does orthography teach ?
What is a letter ?
How many letters in the Alphabet ?
Of what are letters the representatives ?
What is an articulate sound ?
How are letters divided ?
What is a vowel ?
What is a consonant

13

Which letters are the vowels?

Why is *a* a vowel? *Ans.* Because it can be pronounced without the help of any other letter.

Why is *b* a consonant? *Ans.* Because it cannot be pronounced without the help of a vowel.

Which vowel is used in pronouncing *b*? *Ans.* *e.*

Is it placed before, or after the *b*? *Ans.* After it.*

When are *w* and *y* consonants?

What is *w* in the word *wall*? *Ans.* A consonant.

How is it known to be a consonant? *Ans.* By its beginning a word.

What is *w* in the word *new*? *Ans.* A vowel.

How is it known to be a vowel? *Ans.* By its not beginning a word.†

What are the consonants divided into?

Which are the mutes?

Which are the semi-vowels?

Which of of the semi-vowels are called liquids? Why?

ON CHAP. 28.

How many sounds has *B*?‡

How are *GH* sounded?

How are *PH* sounded?

What is said of *Q*?

What sound has *W* when a consonant?

What sound has *Y* when a consonant?

ON CHAP. 29.

What is a diphthong?

What is a proper diphthong?

What is an improper diphthong?

Is there a diphthong in the word *noise*?§

---

* *Similar questions concerning other letters should be asked, and care taken to point out to the pupil particularly how the vowels and consonants are formed by the organs of speech. It is very easy to do this, and very necessary it should be done.*

† *Similar questions should be asked concerning* y.

‡ *This question may be applied to each of the consonants, varying the last letter, except those which are inserted.*

§ *The judicious teacher will see that this, and many of the questions on the 29th chapter, are designed as examplesfor the formation of others, which should be repeated and varied until the scholar thoroughly understand the subject.*

Which letters are the diphthong? *Ans. oi.*
Is it proper, or improper? *Ans.* Proper.
Why is it proper? *Ans.* Because both vowels are sounded.
Is there a diphthong in the word *grain* ?
Which letters are the diphthong? *Ans. ai.*
Is it proper or improper? *Ans.* Improper.
Why is it improper? *Ans.* Because but one vowel is sounded.
What is a triphthong?
Is there a triphthong in the word *adieu* ?
Which letters are the triphthong? *Ans. ieu.*
Which of them is sounded?
What is a syllable ?
What is spelling?
What are words?
What is a word of one syllable termed ?
What is a word of two ?
What is a word of three ?
What is a word of four or more?
What sort of a word is *table* ? *Ans.* A dissyllable.
Why is it called a dissyllable ? *Ans.* Because it has two syllables.
What sort of a word is *orthography*? *Ans.* A polysyllable.
Why is it called a polysyllable? *Ans.* Because it has four syllables.
How many kinds of words are there?
What is a primitive word ?
What is a derivative word?
What is a compound word ?
What sort of a word is *amount?* *Ans.* Primitive.
What sort of word is *distinguishing* ? *Ans.* Derivative.
From what is it derived? *Ans.* From *distinguish.*
What sort of a word is *inkstand* ? *Ans.* A compound word.
Of what is it formed? *Ans.* Of *ink* and *stand.*

ON CHAP. 31.

What is Accent?
Which syllable of the word *grammar* is accented ?
What is Emphasis ?
What is Inflection of the voice ?
What is the *rising* inflection ?
What is the *falling* inflection ?

ON CHAP. 32.

What is Punctuation ?
What are the principal points ?
What is the Comma ?
What is the Semicolon ?

What is the Colon ?   What is the Period ?
What does the Interrogation point show ?
How is the Exclamation point used ?
What does the Parenthesis include ?
What pause and inflection of voice are required by the
  Parenthesis ?
What does the Dash denote ?
What is an accent ?
How many accents are used ?
To what syllables is the grave accent applied ?
To what is the acute applied ?
What is the grave accent also used to denote ?
What is the acute also used to denote ?
What does a Breve show ?
How is a Hyphen used ?
What does a Circumflex denote ?
How is a Diæresis placed ?
How are Brackets used ?
What does a Quotation include?
What is an Apostrophe ?
What does a Caret show ?
What does an Ellipsis show ?
What does an Index point to ?
What does a Paragraph denote ?
How is a Section used ?   How is a Brace used ?
For what are the Asterisk, Obelisk, &c. used ?

HYMN OF THANKSGIVING FOR THE WORKS OF THE CREATOR.

To thee, O Lord! from whom proceed-
eth every blessing, and who dispensest them
so bountifully, to thee belong glory, honour,
and thanksgiving. Thou hearest the cry of
the young raven, and takest pleasure in the
song of the lark ; vouchsafe to listen to my
voice also, and accept the tribute of praise
due to thee. The least of the creatures
formed by thy hand proclaims thy wisdom.
The traces of thy goodness and power are
seen from one end of the year to the other,

and are continually renewing. With paren-
tal tenderness thou providest for our neces-
sities, and givest to men and, animals their
proper food. It is in the hope of thy blessing that the farmer sows his corn : it is thou
who makest the seed fruitful. Thou waterest the furrows of the fields. Thou clothest
the meadow, the valley, and the plain with
flowers and herbage, with trees and groves.
Thou orderest the cool and refreshing dew
to moisten our gardens and fields, and to
shed on them fertility and abundance. The
barren and dry soil thou waterest with gentle rains. The cold and wet places thou
warmest with the rays of the sun. The
weather and the seasons thou orderest in
wisdom, and in the manner most beneficial
to mankind. Thou coverest our fields with
rich harvests, and the wings of the wind
support the waving corn. Thou adornest
the tops of barren rocks with grapes. Thou
dressest our pasture with clover ; and, by
thy command, the fountains and streams water the thirsty animals. Thou causest the
tree to take root and it prospers. A quick-
ening sap circulates through its trunk, and
gives it force to branch out with leaves and
blossoms ; while the abundance of fruit, under which the boughs bend, proves the pleasure which thou hast in doing good. We,
therefore, glorify thee, our Creator, our

13*

Benefactor! We bless thy holy name! All thy works are good, and great, and wonderful. We rejoice in thy goodness.

~~~~~~~~~~~~

CATERPILLARS.

Caterpillars are hatched from the eggs of butterflies. During the winter they remain in an egg state, lifeless; but the same vivifying sun that pushes out the budding leaf and the opening flower, and causes the swelling acorn to give birth to the spreading oak, calls the caterpillar also into life, to share the banquet that nature has provided for her children. Its life, however, seems one continual succession of changes; and, towards the end of summer, after having changed its skin several times, it ceases to eat, and is employed in building a retreat; in which it quits the form of a caterpillar, and assumes that of a butterfly. But the caterpillar, and the butterfly that comes from it, appear to be two very different creatures. The former is a rough and disagreeable reptile; the latter is adorned with the liveliest and most beautiful colours, and distinguished by ornaments which man can never hope to acquire: the former crawled sluggishly on the earth, a mean-looking worm, often in danger of being crushed, and feeding on gross food; while the latter soars to the sky; ranges all the beauties of the creation, himself among the greatest; sports in the sunbeams; displays his golden wings; and needs no other food than the dews of Heaven and the honied juices which are drawn from the flowers. Who is it that hath raised this insect above the earth, enabled it to live in the air, and bestowed upon it such a profusion of beauties? The Maker of the butterfly, and of man—who hath shewn us, in this extraordinary insect, the wonderful change that awaits ourselves; when " this corruptible shall put on incorruption, and this mortal shall put on immortality."

THE STARRY HEAVENS.

Ye sons of men, lift up your eyes,
And view the glories of the skies:
From east to west, from pole to pole,
What orbs on orbs unnumber'd roll!

All know their place, all keep their way,
All move in regular array,
Say! who has made them? who sustains?
Who guides them through the trackless plains?

'Tis He—the everlasting God.
Obedient to his sov'reign nod,
Forth issues the nocturnal host,
And He to each assigns his post.

He calls his army by their names,
Arrays them all with glorious frames;

And night to night his power displays,
And every star resounds his praise.

Investing this terrestrial globe,
Heaven wide expands its azure robe,
All o'er emblaz'd ; that all may see,
Own, and adore, a Deity.

~~~~~~~~~~

A TUTOR TO HIS PUPILS.

THE subsequent poetical fragment was
found in the port-folio of a veteran instructer
of youth : it is short, and therefore its moral
is more striking. The young may possibly
doubt the justice of a maxim, which fascina-
ting hope is fond of veiling from their eyes.
Experience, however, will prove it true.

To you whose days in easy circles flow,
Nor anxious cares, nor guilty passions know ;
Whose ductile souls are studious to improve,
And blend fair learning with your tutor's love,
The Muse devotes her moralizing strain,
And speaks this long-tried truth—" that Life
            is vain ;"
That half our years are sunk in sorrow's
            shade ;
That scarce we blossom—ere we're doom'd
            to fade ;
That Virtue, sole, illumes our darksome road,
And guides through danger to the throne of
            God.

A select, Collection of Words,

WITH BRIEF DEFINITIONS.

Note. A vowel ending a syllable, with the accent on it, is long. When a consonant ends an accented syllable, the preceding vowel is short. When *I* precedes *cian, cial, cient, cion, cious, gious, tial, tion,* and *tious,* it is short. Proper diphthongs are not marked. Vowels otherwise circumstanced are marked.

A ban'don, to give up, forsake
A base', to cast down.
A bate', to lessen.
Ab bre'vi ate, to shorten.
Ab bre vi a'tion, act of short-
　ening, characters signify-
　ing whole words.
Ab hor', to hate.
A bide', to remain in a place
A bil'i ty, power to do any
　thing.
A bode', place of residence.
A bol'ish, to annul.
A bom'in a ble, hateful.
A bove', higher, overhead.
A breast', side by side.
Ab solve', to clear, to acquit
　of a crime.
Ab surd', inconsistent
A bun'dant, plentiful.
A byss', depth without bot-
　tom.　　　　　[cation.
A cad'e my, a place for edu-
Ac cent'u al, relating to ac-
　cent.　　　　　[cent.
Ac cent'u ate, to place the ac-
Ac'ci dent, casualty, chance
Ac count', computation.
Ac cou' tre (ac coo' tur), to
　dress, to equip.　　[page.
Ac cou'tre ment, dress, equi-
Ac'cu ra cy, exactness.
Ac'cu rate, exact.
Ac'cu rate ly, exactly.
Ac cu sa'tion, act of accusing.
Ac cus'tom, to habituate.

Ace, a unit on cards or dice.
Ache, to be in pain.
A chieve', to perform.
Ac'id, sharp, sour.
A'corn, the seed of the oak.
Ac quaint', to make familiar
　with.
Ac quire, to gain by labour.
A'cre (a'kur) 160 square rods
　of land.
Ac'tu ate, to put in action.
A cute', sharp　　　[cious.
Ad he'sive, sticking, tena-
A dieu', farewell. [other day.
Ad journ', to put off to an-
Ad'mi ra ble, to be admired.
Ad mi ra'tion, wonder.
Ad mis'sion, admittance.
Ad mon'ish, to reprove gently
Ad mo ni'tion, gentle reproof.
A do'ra ble, that which should
　be adored.
A do ra'tion, divine worship.
Ad ver'si ty, affliction, calam-
　ity.　　　　　[tion.
Ad ver' tise ment, informa-
Ad vise', to counsel, to inform
Ad'vo cate, he that pleads
Af fec'tion, love, kindness
Af'firm, to assert confidently
Af fo rd', to yield.
Af front', insult, outrage.
A'gen cy, business of an agent.
Ag'gran dize, to make great.
Ag griev'ance, injury, wrong.
A ghast', struck with horror.

Ag'o ny, excessive pain.

A gree'ment, concord, re-semblance.   [bandry.

Ag' ri cul ture, tillage, hus-

A'gue, an intermittent fever.

Al'i ment, nourishment, food.

Al low'ance, sanction, sum granted.

âl ma nack, a calendar. [poor.

àlms'house, a hospital for the

Al'pha bet, the letters in any language.   [things.

Al'ter'na tive, choice of two

Al'ti tude, height of a place.

âl'ways, perpetually. [ment.

Am bi'tion, desire of prefer-

A'mi a ble, lovely, pleasant.

Am'i ca ble, friendly.

A miss', faulty, criminally.

Am mu ni' tion, military stores.   [ers.

A móng', mingled with oth-

Am' or ous, inclined to love.

Am' pu tate, to cut off a limb.

A muse'ment, entertainment.

An a log' ic al, pertaining to analogy,   [ment.

An'ar chy, want of govern-

A nat'o my, the art of dis-secting the body.

ăn' cient, old.

An' ger, passion, rage. [ger.

An' gry, tormented with an-

A ni mal, a living creature.

An i mat ed, lively, vigorous.

An' nu al, yearly.   [name.

A non' y mous, wanting a

An' swer, a reply to a ques-tion.

An te ce' dent, going before.

An' them, a sacred song.

An'ti dote, a medicine to ex-pel poison.   [antiquities.

An ti qua' ri an, relative to

A part' ment, a room, a set of rooms

Ap' er ture, an open place.

Aph' o rism, a maxim.

A pol' o gy, defence, excuse.

Ap pa ra'tus, tools, furniture.

Ap par' el, dress, clothing.

Ap pa' rent, evident, plain.

Ap pa ri' tion, a spectre.

Ap pear', to be in sight.

Ap pear' ance, the coming into sight.

Ap pel' lant, one that ap-peals from a lower to a higher pow er.   [cused.

Ap pel lee', one who is ac-

Ap' pe tite, natural desire.

Ap point' ment, establish-ment.   [value.

Ap pre' ci ate, to rate, to

Ap pre hend', to lay hold on.

Ap proach', to draw near.

Ap pro' pri ate, peculiar.

A' pri cot, a kind of wall [fruit.

A'que ous, watery.

Ar' a ble, fit for tillage.

Arc, a segment of a circle.

Arch, a part of a circle.

Arch ăn' gel, one of the high-est order of angels.

Arch bish' op, chief bishop.

Ar' chi tect, one skilled in building.

Ar gu men ta'tion, reasoning.

Ar' id, dry, parched up.

Ar ith' me tic, the science of numbers.

Ar' mour, defensive arms.

Ar o mat' ic, spicy, fragrant,

Ar raign', to bring to trial.

Ar range' ment, state of be-ing put in order.

Ar rest', to seize by law.

Ar'ro gance, pride, presump-tion   [distinctly.

Ar tic'u late, to form words

Ar' ti fice, trick, stratagem.

As cribe', to attribute to.

As' pe rate, to make rough.
As' pi rate, to pronounce full.
As sas' sin, a murderer.
As sume', to claim, to take.
As sure (*as shure'*) to make secure.
As sess' ment, a sum levied.
As sign ee', one appointed, or deputed.
As suage', to mitigate.
As'te risk, a mark in printing.
Asth' ma, a disease.
As ton' ish ment, amazement.
A sy' lum, a refuge. [God.
A' the ism, the disbelief of a
At' las, a book of maps.
At tend', to wait on.
At ten' tion, act of attending.
At test', to witness.
At tor' ney, a lawyer, an agent
Av'a rice, covetousness.
Au' burn, brown.
Au' di ence, act of hearing.
Au' di to ry, persons assembled to hear.
Aug ment', to increase.
A void', to escape, [weight.
Av our du pois', a kind of
Aus tere', severe, harsh.
Au thor' i ty, power, influence.
Au' tumn, a part of the year.
Awk' ward, unpolite, un- [taught.
Axe, an edged tool.
Ax'le tree, that on which the wheels of a carriage turns.
Ay (*ăē*) yes.
A' zure, faint blue.
B.
Bach'e lor, a man unmarried.
Baize, a kind of coarse cloth.
Bal' ance, to make equal.
Bal' lot, a ticket.
Balm, the name of a plant.
Bal' sam, ointment, unguent.
Ban ish ment, state of being banished.

Ban' quet, to feast, fare dain- [tily.
Ban' ter, to play upon.
Bar ba' ri an, a man without pity.
Bar'ba rous, savage, cruel.
Bar' ber, a man who shaves the beard.
Barge, a boat for pleasure.
Bar' ley, a kind of grain.
Bar' on, a degree of nobility.
Bar' ri er, obstruction, limit.
Bass vi' ol, a musical instrument.
Bas' i lisk, a kind of serpent.
Ba' sin, a small vessel.
Ba' sis, the foundation. [ment.
Bas soon', a musical instru-
Bat tal' ion, a division of an army. [the end of a gun.
Bay' on et, a short sword on
Beak, the bill of a bird.
Beard, hair on the lips and chin.
Beast, an irrational animal.
Beav' er, an animal.
Beau' ti ful, fair.
Beaux, (*boze*) *plural of* bean.
Be come', to fit, to adorn.
Bee' tle, an insect, a heavy mallet. [alms.
Beg' gar, one who lives upon
Be guile', to impose upon.
Be hold' er, a spectator.
Be lief', faith, religion.
Be moan', to lament.
Ben e dic' tion, a blessing.
Be nef' i cent, kind, doing good.
Ben' e fit, favour, profit.
Be nev' o lence, kindness, charity.
Be queath', to leave by will
Be reave', to deprive of.
Be seech', to intreat, to implore.
Be set', to fall upon.
Be siege', to lay siege to

156   *A select Collection of Words.*

Be stow', to give, confer.
Bev' er age, liquor to drink.
Be wāil', to lament.
Big'ot ry, blind zeal.
Bill' iards, a kind of play.
Bi og' ra phy, a book of lives.
Blame' less, guiltless.
Blem' ish, a deformity.
Blend, to mix.   [licity.
Bles' sed ness, heavenly fe-
Bles' sing, divine favour.
Blind, without sight.
Blithe'some, gay, cheerful.
Bloom'-ing, yielding blos-
   soms.   [plant.
Blos' som, the flower of a
Blun' der, a gross mistake.
Bo hea', a species of tea.
Bom bas' tic, high sounding.
Bon' net, a hat or cap.
Bot' a nist, one skilled in
   plants.
Boun' te ous, liberal, kind.
Brain' less, silly.
Bra va'do, a boast, a brag.
Bra' ve ry, courage
Breeze, a gentle gale.
Bri'dal, nuptial.   [man.
Bride'groom, a new married
Bright' ness, lustre, splen-
   dour.   [dour.
Brill' ian cy, lustre, splen-
Brisk'ness, liveliness.
Brŏnze, brass.
Brook, a running water.
Buck' ler, a shield.
Build'ing, an edifice. [guage.
Bur lesque', ludicrous lan-
Būsh'el, thirty-two quarts.
Busi' ness, (*biz ness*) employ-
   ment.
But' ter fly, a beautiful insect.
     C.
Ca'dence, fall of the voice.
Ca det', a volunteer in an
   army.   [wretched.
Ca lam'-i tous, unhappy,

Cal'cu late, to compute.
Càlf, young of a cow. [ton.
Cal' i co, cloth made of cot-
Câlk, to stop the leaks of a
   ship.
Ca lum' ni ate, to slander.
Cām' bric, fine linen, or cot-
   ton cloth.   [receive.
Ca' pa ble, sufficient, able to
Cap'it al, head, chief.
Ca pit' u late, to surrender.
Cap' tain, an officer.
Cap' tive, one taken in war.
Car' ri on, flesh corrupted.
Cas' cade, a water fall.
Cas' si a, a sweet spice.
Cat' a logue, a list.
Ca tàrrh', a disease in the
   head.
Ca tas' tro phe, an event.
Cat' e chise, to question, to
   examine.   [worm.
Cat'er pil lar, an insect, a
Cave, a cavern.
Cau'tion, prudence, warning.
Cel'i ba cy, single life.
Cen' sure, blame, reproach.
Cer e mo'ni al, formal.
Chām'ber, an apartment in a
   house.   [of goat.
Cha mois', (*sham moy'*) a kind
Cham' pi on, a single combat-
   ant.
Chance, fortuitous event.
Chan' dler, one who makes
   candles.
Chānge, alteration, novelty.
Chānge a ble, fickle, uncer-
Cha'os, confusion.   [tain.
Chap' el, place of worship.
Chap'ter, a division of a book.
Char'-ac ter ize, to give a
   character.   [sure
Ch a'i ot, a carriage for plea-
Char'it a ble, kind in giving.
Char'i ty, tenderness, love,
Chas m, a cleft, agap. [alms

Chas·tise', to punish.

Chas' tise ment, punishment.

Cheap'ness, lowness of price.

Cheek, side of the face.

Cheer'less, without gayety.

Cheese, food made of milk.

Cher' ub, a celestial spirit.

Cher'u bim, *plural of* cherub.

Chief'ly, principally.

Chil'ly, somewhat cold.

Choir(*kwire*) a band of singers

Cho'ral, sung by a choir.

Christ'en, to baptize.

Chris'tian, a follower of Christ.   [at baptism.

Chris'tian name, name given

Chro nol'o gy, science of computing time.

Churn, to make butter.

Ci'der, juice of apples.

Cin'na mon, a spice.

Cinque, five on dice.

Ci'on, a sprout used in graft- ing fruit trees.   [tic.

Ci'pher, to practise arithme-

Cit'i zen, a freeman.

Claim, a demand.

Clam'our, outcry, noise.

Clar'i fy, to purify.

Clar'ion, a trumpet.

Clean'ness, neatness.

Clear'ness, brightness.

Clem'en cy, mercy.

Cler'gy, a body of divines.

Clerk'ship, the office of a clerk.

Clock, an instrument to mea- sure time.

Clos'et, a small room.

Clown'ish, ill-bred, clumsy.

Co a lesce', to unite.

Coax, to wheedle, to flatter.

Co'coa, a kind of nut.

Co e'qual, equal with.

Co e'val, cotemporary.

Cof'fee, a plant.

14

Co'gent, convincing.

Coin, money stamped.

Co in cide', to concur.

Col'league, a partner.

Col'lege, a house of learning.

Col'o ny, a plantation from the mother country.

Col'our, appearance, hue.

Com bine', to join, to agree.

Com bin'ed, joined.

Com'et, a blazing star.

Com'fort, ease, pleasure.

Com'ic al, diverting.

Com mand'er, a chief.

Com mence', to begin.

Com mis'sion, a warrant of office.

Com mis'sion er, one empow- ered to act.

Com'mo dore, a captain who commands a squadron.

Com mu'ni cant, one who receives the Lord's supper.

Com pan'ion, an associate.

Com par'a tive, capable of being compared.

Com pas'sion, sympathy.

Com pel', to force.

Com'pend, an abridgment.

Com'pe tent, qualified.

Com pi'ler, one who frames a composition from various authors.

Com pla'cen cy, gratification.

Com plaint', remonstrance.

Com plai sance', desire of pleasing.   [pleasing.

Com plai sant', desirous of

Com plex'ion, colour of the face.

Com pli'ant, yielding.

Com pose', to put together.

Con'cave, hollow.

Con ceit', idea, fancy.

Con ceit ed, proud.

Con'clave, a close assembly.

Con clud ed, finished.

Con cur' rnece, combination, help. [ishment.

Con demn', to doom to pun-

Con de scend', to stoop, to yield.

Con dole', to lament with.

Con' duit, a pipe for convey- ing water.

Con y, (*cun'ne*) a rabbit.

Con fec'tion er, one who sells sweetmeats.

Con fed er a' tion, alliance.

Con fes' sion, acknowledg- ment.

Con'fi dence, assurance, trust.

Con fine' ment, restraint of liberty. [proof

Con fir ma' tion, evidence,

Con fla gra'tion, a general fire

Con' flict, a combat.

Con form' i ty, resemblance.

Con found', to perplex, to astonish.

Con geal', to freeze.

Con grat' u late, to wish joy.

Con gre ga' tion, an assembly.

Con' gress, legislature of the U. S. [cone.

Con' ic, having the form of a

Con jec'ture, guess, notion.

Con' ju gal, matrimonial.

Con' ju gate, to inflect verbs.

Con junc' tion, union, a part of speech.

Con ju ra'tion, enchantment.

Con nect', to join, to link,

Con nex'ion, relation, union.

Con nois seur, (*co nes sare'*) a critic.

Con' quer, to get the victory.

Con san guin'i ty, relation by blood. [pulous.

Con sci en' tious, just, scru-

Con' se quence, effect.

Con' serve, a sweetmeat.

Con sid er, to examine.

Con sist' ent, conformable.

Con so la' tion, comfort.

Con spic' u ous, easy to be seen.

Cón' sta ble, a peace officer.

Con' stan cy, firmness.

Con' stant, free from change of affection. [stars.

Con stel la' tion, a cluster of

Con stit' u ent, an elector.

Con straint', compulsion.

Con sult', to ask advice.

Con sume', to waste away.

Con sump' tion, act of con- suming.

Con'tact, touch.

Con ta' gi ous, infectious.

Con tem' plate, to meditate.

Con tem' po ra ry, living in the same age.

Con ten' tion, debate, strife.

Con tent' ment, satisfaction.

Con tin' u al, incessant.

Con tin'u al ly, without ceas- ing.

Con tor' tion, wry motion.

Con tour, (*con toor'*) the out- line.

Con tra dic' tion, opposition.

Con' tra ry, opposite.

Con tri bu' tion, act of con- tributing.

Con tri' tion, penitence.

Con' tro ver sy, dispute, quarrel.

Con va les' cent, recovering.

Con' ver sant, familiar.

Con ver sa' tion, familiar dis- course.

Con ver'sion, change of state.

Con' vex, rising in a circular form. [send to.

Con vey (*con va'*) to carry, to

Co nun' drum, a low jest.

Con vul' sion, a violent mo- tion.

Co' pi ous, plentiful.

Cor po' re al, having a body.

Corpse, a dead body.

Cor rect', accurate. [rupted.
Cor rup'ti ble, may be cor-
Cor rup' tion, wickedness, putrescence.
Cos mop'o lite, a citizen of the world. [same time.
Co tem'po ra ry, living at the
Cóv' e nant, a contract.
Cóv' et ous, avaricious.
Cóv' et ous ness, avarice.
Coun'sel lor, one that gives advice. [gery.
Coun'ter feit, deceitful,a for-
Coun' ter pane, a coverlet for a bed.
Coup' let, a pair of rhymes.
Cour'te ous, well bred.
Cow'ard ice, want of courage
Cre a'tion, act of creating.
Cre a' tor, the Deity.
Crea' ture, a thing created.
Cred'it or, he that gives cre-dit.
Cred' u lous, unsuspecting.
Cres' cent, the moon in her increase.
Crim' son, deep red.
Cri' sis, a critical time.
Crit' i cism, censure, remark.
Cru' el, inhuman.
Crup' per, part of a saddle.
Crush, to squeeze.
Crys' tal, a pellucid stone.
Crys' tal lize, to shoot into crystals. [sides
Cube, a body of six equal
Cu' bit, about 18 inches.
Cu'cum ber, a plant and fruit.
Cul'ti va tion, improvement.
Cu ri os' i ty, inquisitiveness.
Cur'tain, a cloth expanded or contracted at pleasure.
Cur' va ture, crookedness.
Cush' ion, a soft seat.

D.

Dag' ger, a short sword.
Dain' ti ly, delicately.

Dai' sy, a flower.
Dam' age, mischief, loss.
Dam' sel, a young woman.
Dam'son, a small black plum.
Dān' ger, hazard, peril.
Das'tard, a coward. [light.
Daz'zle, to overpower with
Dea' con, a church officer.
Death, extinction of life.
Death'watch, a small insect.
De bark', to disembark.
De bil'i ty, weakness.
Dec'a logue, the ten com-mandments.
De cep' tion, fraud.
Dec'i mal, numbered by tens.
De ci'pher, to explain.
De clen' sion, inflection of nouns.
De cliv'i ty, gradual descent.
De co' rous, decent, suitable,
Ded' i cate, to devote.
De fal ca'tion, diminution.
De fault', neglect.
De fec' tion, apostacy.
Def'er ence, respect, regard.
De fi' cient, failing, wanting.
De file', a narrow passage.
De fine', to explain.
De fin' ing, explaining.
Def' in ite, certain, limited.
De form', to disfigure.
De fraud' er, a deceiver.
De' i ty, a divinity, a GOD.
De jec' tion, lowness of spir-its.
De lay', to put off, to hinder.
Del' e gate, a deputy.
De lib' er ate, to think in or-der to choice.
Del' i cate, fine, nice,
De light', joy, pleasure.
De lude', to beguile.
Del' uge, inundation.
De mand', a claim.
De mean'our, behaviour.
De mise', death, decease.

De' mon, an evil spirit.

Den, a cavern.

De nom' in ate, to name.

De note', to betoken.

Dens e, close, compact.

De ny', to refuse.

De part'ure, a going away.

De plore', to lament.

De pop' u late, to lay waste.

De pos' ite, a trust, a pledge.

De prav' i ty, corruption.

De pre' ci ate, to undervalue.

De pres' sion, a sinking, or falling.

Dep' u ty, one that transacts business for another.

De riv' a tive, derived from another. [parage.

Der' o gate, to lessen, to dis-

De scend', to come down.

De scent', declivity, offspring.

De scrip' tion, act of describ-

De sign', intention. [ing.

De spise', to contemn.

Des' pot, an absolute prince.

De ter'min ed, decided, come to an end.

De test', to abhor.

De vas ta' tion, destruction.

De vi a' tion, a swerving.

De vice', contrivance, emblem.

De void', empty, vacant.

De vout', pious.

Di aer' e sis,* this mark (··).

Dic' tion a ry, a book of words explained in alphabetical order.

Dif' fer ence, disagreement.

Dif'fer ent, unlike, dissimilar.

Dif'fi cul ty, hardness, objection.

Di men' sion, capacity, bulk.

Di rec' tion, order.

Dirge, a mournful ditty.

Dis a gree', to differ.

Dis a gree' a ble, unpleasing.

Dis ap point' ment, defeat of hopes.

Dis as'ter, misfortune.

Dis cern, (diz zern') to distinguish, to see.

Dis charge', to release.

Dis ci' ple, a scholar. [fort.

Dis con'so late, without com-

Dis course', conversation.

Dis creet', prudent.

Dis cuss', to examine.

Dis dain', to scorn.

Dis hon' est, void of probity.

Dis'lo cate, to put out of joint.

Dis mis'sion, sending away.

Dis o be' di ence, breach of

Dis perse', to scatter. [duty.

Dis play', to exhibit.

Dis please', to offend.

Dis seize', to dispossess.

Dis sem i na'tion, act of scattering.

Dis ser ta'tion, a discourse.

Dis'so lute, loose, wanton.

Dis tem'per, a disease.

Dis tin' guish ed, eminent.

Di ver' sion, sport, amusement. [things.

Di vin' i ty, science of divine

Di vis'ion, a dividing, a partition.

Dol' lar, 100 cents.

Dol' phin, a fish.

Do na' tion, thing given.

Doub'le, twofold.

Dow' er, a wife's portion.

Dox ol'o gy, a form of giving glory to God.

Drag oon', a horse soldier.

Draught, act of drinking.

Drow' si ness, sleepiness.

Du' el, a fight between two.

Du o dec' i mo, a book in which a sheet makes 12 leaves.

* *i* in first long.

Du plic' i ty, deceit.
Du ra' tion, continuance.

E.

Ear 'nest ness, eagerness.
Earth, the world. [earth.
Earth' quake, tremor of the
Echo, a sound returned.
E con'o my, frugality.
Ed'u cate, to bring up.
Eke, to supply, to spin out.
E lapse', to pass away.
E las' tic, springy.
E lec'tion, choice.
El'e ment, a first principle.
El e ment'a ry, not compounded.
El e va' tion, exaltation.
El o cu' tion, eloquence.
Em bar'go, prohibition to sail.
Em bar' rass, to perplex.
Em' bas sy, a public message.
Em'bry o, any thing unfinished.
E met' ic, provoking vomits.
E mo' tion, disturbance of mind. [busy.
Em ploy', to exercise, to
Em ploy' ment, business.
Em pow' er, to authorize.
Em u la'tion, rivalry, contest.
En chant'ment, excessive delight.
En clos'ure, space enclosed.
En coun'ter, sudden meeting.
En cour'age, to embolden.
En dorse'ment, writing on the
En'e my, a foe. [back.
E nig'ma, a riddle.
En gage', to enter upon.
Eng lish (ing'glish) belonging
to England. [tion.
En large'ment, augmenta-
En rol', to register.
En' ter, to go into.
En ter tain', to amuse.
En tomb', to put into a tomb.

14*

En'vy, vexation at another's prosperity.
E pis'tle, a letter.
E pit'o me, an abridgment.
E quip', to furnish.
Eq'ui ty, justice, right.
Er ro'ne ous, mistaking.
Er' rour, blunder, mistake.
Er u di'tion, learning.
E scape', to avoid.
E spouse', to betroth.
Es sen' tial, important.
E ter' nal, without beginning
or end. [the gospel.
E van' ge lize, to instruct in
E'ven ing, close of the day.
Ev er last'ing, perpetual.
Ev'i dence, testimony.
Eu'lo gy, praise, encomium.
Eu ro pe' an, belonging to
Europe. [ing.
Ex am in a'tion, a question-
Ex am' ple, an instance to
prove by.
Ex as' pe rate, to provoke.
Ex cep' tion, objection.
Ex cite', to rouse, to animate.
Ex cu' sa ble, pardonable.
Ex e cu' tion, performance.
Ex ec' u tor, one who performs the will of another.
Ex' ile, banishment.
Ex ot' ic, foreign.
Ex pe' di ent, proper, conve-
Ex'pe dite, to hasten. [nient.
Ex pire', to die, to conclude.
Ex pla na' tion, interpreta-
Ex pose', to lay open. [tion.
Ex po si' tion, explanation.
Ex'quis ite, excellent.
Ex tem' po re, without premeditation.
Ex tend', to stretch out.
Ex tin'guish, to put out.
Ex traor' di na ry, more than
common.
Ex trav'a gant, irregular.

F.

Fa' ble, a moral fiction.
Fa ce' tious, gay, cheerful.
Fa cil' i tate, to make easy in the doing.
Fac'tor, an agent for another.
Fāith, belief, trust, fidelity.
Fâl'chion, a short sword.
Fal la' cious, deceitful.
Fâlse'hood, a lie. [known.
Fa mil' iar, affable, well-
Fan tas' tic, whimsical.
Fas' ci nate, to enchant.
Fash' ion, form, custom.
FATH' om, six feet.
Fault, a defect, an offence.
Fa' vour, kindness.
Fear'ful, timorous.
Fear' less, intrepid.
Fee'ble ness, weakness.
Fe lic' i tate, to congratulate.
Fe ro' cious, savage, fierce.
Fer til' i ty, fruitfulness.
Fer' vent, ardent.
Fes tiv' i ty, joyfulness.
Fet' ters, chains for the feet.
Fick' le, inconstant.
Fic' tion, falsehood.
Fil' ial, pertaining to a son.
Fi' nal, last, conclusive.
Fi' ne ry, show, splendour.
Fi nesse', stratagem.
Fi' nite, limited.
Fire' lock, a soldier's gun.
Firm'ness, stability.
Flag'e let, a small flute.
Flat' ter, to praise falsely.
Fleece, the wool of one
Flex'i ble, pliant. [sheep.
Flight, act of flying.
Flip' pant, talkative.
Fluc'tu ate, to be irresolute.
Fod'der, dry food for cattle.
Fo'li age, leaves.
Fo'li o, a book in which a sheet makes two leaves.
Fop' pe ry, fondness of dress.

For bid', to prohibit.
Fōr'ci ble, strong, violent.
Fore'head, upper part of the face. [nate·
Foie or dain', to predesti-
For feit, a fine.
For get', to neglect. [tion.
Fōr'ge ry, crime of falsifica-
For give', to pardon.
For mal'i ty, ceremony.
Fōrth with', immediately.
For' ti tude, bravery.
For'tu nate, successful.
Foun' tain, a first cause.
Frac'tion, part of an integer.
Fra'grant, odorous.
Frank'ness, openness.
Fra ter' nal, brotherly.
Free' dom, liberty.
Fre'quent ly, repeatedly.
Fret'ful ness, peevishness.
Friend, a familiar compan-ion.
Friend'ship, union of minds.
Frock, outside garment.
Fro'ward, peevish, perverse.
Fru gal' i ty, good husban-
Ful' some, nauseous. [dry.
Fu'ne ral, interment.
Fu' ri ous, mad, raging.
Fur'lough, leave of absence.
Fur' long, forty rods.
Fur' row, a long trench.
Fu tu' ri ty, time to come.

G.

Gai'ly, cheerfully.
Gain'say, to contradict.
Gal'ax y, the milky way.
Gal'lan try, bravery.
Gal'lon, four quarts.
Game, a single match at play.
Gaol (*jale*), a prison.
Gàr'den, a place to raise plants. [ers.
Gàr'land, a wreath of flow-
Gāuge, a measure, a standard
Gem, a jewel.

Gen e al' o gy, a history of family descents.

Gen er a'tion, an age, proge- [ny.

Gen'er ous, munificent.

Gen teel', polite, elegant.

Gen'tle man, a term of complaisance.

Gen'u ine, not spurious.

Ge og'ra phy, knowledge of the earth.

Ges'ture, action, posture.

Ghäst'ly, like a ghost.

Gi'ant, one unnaturally tall and large.

Gid di ness, inconstancy.

Gi gan'tic, bulky, enormous.

Gin'ger, a plant and root.

Gip'sy, a vagabond.

Gla'zier, one who makes glass windows.

Globe, a sphere.

Glo'ri ous, illustrious.

Glo'ry, honour, praise, fame.

Glos'sa ry, a dictionary of obscure or antiquated words explained.

Glut'ton y, excess of eating.

Goal, a starting post.

Gob'let, a bowl, or cup.

Gob'lin, an evil spirit.

Gon'do la, a large flat boat.

Gos'ling, a young goose.

Gov'ern, to regulate.

Gov'ern our, one who has supreme authority in a state.

Grace, favour, pardon, effect of God's influence.

Gra'cious, merciful. [gress.

Gra da'tion, a regular pro-

Grap'nel, a small anchor.

Gra'tis, without reward.

Grat'i tude, duty to benefactors.

Grave, place for the dead.

Grav'i ty, weight, seriousness.

Gra'zier, one who feeds cattle

Greed'i ness, hunger.

Gren a dier', a tall foot soldier.

Grieve, to mourn, to sorrow.

Grim al' kin, an old cat.

Gro tesque', distorted.

Growl, to snarl, to murmur.

Growth, increase.

Grudge, ill-will, envy.

Guard, to defend.

Guar' di an, one who has the charge of an orphan.

Guess, supposition.

Guit àr', a musical instrument

Gut'tur al, pronounced in the throat.

H.

Hab it a'tion, place of abode.

Ha bit'u al, customary.

Had'dock, a kind of fish.

Hail'stone, a particle of hail.

Hal le lu jah (*hal le loo' yah*) praise ye the Lord.

Hand' i craft, manual occupation.

Hand'some, beautiful.

Hap'pi ness, felicity.

Hap'py, in a state of felicity.

Har angue', a popular oration

Hàr' bour, a port or haven.

Hàr'le quin, a buffoon.

Harm, damage.

Hàr'mo ny, just proportion.

Hàrp' si chord, a musical instrument.

Hās'ty, quick, speedy.

Hatch'et, a small axe.

Hate, to abhor.

Ha'tred, ill-will.

Hat, a cover for the head.

Hat'ter, a maker of hats.

Haugh' ti ness, pride, arrogance.

Haut boy, (*ho'boy*) a musical instrument.

Head'strong, ungovernable.

Health'ful, wholesome.

Health'y, free from sickness

Hĕarse, a carriage for the dead.

Heaᴛн'en, pagans.

Heav'en, the habitation of the blessed.

Heed'less, negligent.

Heir'ess,* a woman who inherits.

Helm, a rudder.

Helve, handle of an axe.

Hem'is phere, half of a globe.

Hep'ta gon, a figure of seven sides.

Herb'age, grass.

Herds'man, a keeper of herds

Her'it age, inheritance.

Her'mit, a solitary.

He'ro, a man eminent for bravery.

Hes'i tate, to pause.

Hex'a gon, a figure of six sides.

Hid'e ous, dreadful, horrible.

High way', a public road.

Hin'der ance, impediment.

His to'ri an, a writer of history.

His'to ry, a narration of facts.

Hoar'y, grey with age.

Hoe, a farming tool.

Ho'li ness, sanctity.

Hŏl'ster, a case for pistols.

Hom'age, service, respect.

Hom'i cide, manslaying.

Hon'est, upright.

Hon'es ty, justice, truth.

Hon'i ed, drawn from flowers.

Hon'our a ble, illustrious.

Ho ri'zon, the line that terminates the view.

Hor i zon'tal, on a level.

Hor'rour, terrour, shuddering.

Hos'pi ta ble, kind to strangers.

Host'ler, one who takes care [of horses.

House'hold, a family.

*ei like a long.

Hu'man, belonging to man.

Hu mane', kind, benevolent.

Hu man'i ty, tenderness.

Hum'ble, not proud.

Hu mil'i ty, submission.

Hu'mor ous, pleasant, jocular.

Hunt'er, one who chases animals.

Hur'ri cane, a violent tempest

Hus'band, a married man.

Hy per'bo le, an exaggeration.

Hyp'o crite, a dissembler in religion.

Hys'sop, (hiz zup) a plant.

I.

I'ci cle, a shoot of ice hanging down.

I de'a, mental imagination.

I dent'ic al, the same.

Id'i ot, a fool.

I'dle ness, laziness.

I dol'a try, the worship of images.

Ig'no min y, disgrace.

Ig no ra'mus, a foolish fellow.

Ig'no rant, untaught.

Il le'gal, contrary to law.

Il lit'er ate, unlettered.

Il lu'min ate, to enlighten.

Il lus'trate, to explain.

Il lus'tri ous, conspicuous.

Im'age, idea, idol, likeness.

Im ag in a'tion, fancy, idea.

Im'i tate, to copy.

Im ma ture', not ripe.

Im me'di ate ly, instantly.

Im men'si ty, infinity. [ter.

Im merse', to put under water.

Im mod'est, indelicate.

Im mor'al, wicked, dishonest.

Im mor'tal, exempt from death. [death.

Im mor tal'i ty, without death.

Im par'tial, equitable.

Im pa'tient ly, eagerly.

Im pen'i tent, obdurate.

Im per fec'tion, defect.

Im pi'e ty, irreverence.

Im' pi ous, wicked, profane.

Im plore', to solicit.

Im por' tant, momentous.

Im prob' a ble, unlikely.

Im pro pri'e ty, unfitness.

Im prop'er, not just, unfit.

Im pru' dence, indiscretion.

Im'pu dent, shameless.

Im' pulse, communicated force. [ing questions.

In ter rog'a tive, used in ask-

Im pure', unholy, foul.

In a bil'i ty, want of power.

In ac' tive, indolent.

In at ten'tion, disregard, neg-

In ca' pa ble, unable. [lect.

In cis' ion, a wound.

In cline', to bend, to lean.

In clude', to comprehend.

In com'pe tent, not adequate.

In con sid'er ate, thoughtless.

In con'stant, changeable.

In cor po' re al, immaterial.

In cor rect', not exact.

In cor rupt', pure, honest.

In cor rup' tion, incapable of corruption. [ited.

In cred'i ble, not to be cred-

In cu ba'tion, the act of set- ting upon eggs. [debt.

In debt'ed, having incurred a

In de pend' ence, freedom from control.

In de pend'ent, free.

In dif'fer ent, unconcerned.

In'di gence, poverty.

In dig'nant, angry.

In dis cre' tion, imprudence.

In dis tinct', confused.

In'do lence, laziness.

In dulge', to favour.

In dul'gent, kind, favourable.

In' dus try, diligence.

In es' ti ma ble, invaluable.

In ex pe'di ent, inconvenient.

In'fant, a child, a babe.

In fec'tion, contagion.

In'fi del, an unbeliever.

In' fi nite, unbounded.

In flec'tion, act of bending or varying. [ment.

In flict', to impose as punish-

In'flu ence, ascendant power

In form', to instruct.

In ge'ni ous ly, wittily, sub- tilly.

In gen'u ous ly, openly, fairly.

In hab'it, to dwell in.

In he'rent, existing in.

In her' it ance, patrimony.

In hu' man, barbarous.

In i tial (*in ish' al*,) placed at the beginning.

In ju'ri ous, mischievous.

In'ju ry, mischief.

In jus' tice, iniquity, wrong.

Inn'hold er, a man who keeps an inn. [ty.

In'no cence, purity, integri-

In quis 'i tive, curious.

In' sect, a small animal.

In sen'si ble, imperceptible.

In sert', to place among oth- er things.

In sin cer'i ty, dissimulation.

In snare', to entangle, to en- trap,

In'so lence, haughtiness.

In sol' vent, unable to pay.

In sta bil' i ty, inconstancy.

In' stant ly, immediately.

In' stinct, the power which determines the will of brutes.

In struct'er, a teacher.

In'stru ment, a tool, an agent.

In' te ger, the whole of any ;thing.

In ten' tion, a design.

In ten'tion al ly, by prior de- sign.

In'ter est ing, affecting.

In ter mis'sion, pause.

In ter' pret, to explain.

In'ter view, mutual sight.

In'ti ma cy, close familiarity.
In tox i ca'tion, drunkenness.
In trep id, fearless, daring.
In trude',* to come uninvited
In ven'tion, discovery. [down.
In vert' ed, turned upside
In vest'ing, inclosing.
In vis' i ble, not to be seen.
Irk' some, weary.
Ir reg'u lar, immethodical.
Ir re li'gion, impiety.
I tin'er ant, wandering.

J.

Jail, a prison.
Jaun'dice, a distemper.
Jeal' ous, suspicious.
Jeop' ar dy, danger, hazard, peril.
Joc'u lar, used in jest.
Jo'vi al, merry, gay, lively.
Ju di'cious, prudent, wise.
Judge, one who presides in a court of judicature.
Judg'ment, decision, opinion.
Jug'gler, a cheat.
Junc' ture, critical time.
Ju' ni or, younger than an-
other. [a cause.
Ju' ry, persons sworn to try
Jus'tice, equity, right.

K.

Keen' ness, sharpness.
Kid'nap, to steal human be-
ings.
Kind'ly, benevolently.
Kind'ness, benevolence.
Kin'dred, affinity.
Kins'man, a relative.
Kite, a bird, a paper bird, or flying figure for amuse-
ment.
Kna' ve ry, dishonesty.
Knit'ter, one who knits.
Knock'er, a hammer which hangs on a door.
Know'ing, skilful.

* u like o middle.

Knowl'edge, certain percep-
tion.

L.

La bo' ri ous, diligent.
La'bour, pain, toil, work.
La'bour er, one who labours.
Lab'y rinth, maze.
Lam en ta'tion, expression of sorrow. [country.
Land'scape, prospect of a
Lan' guage, human speech, tongue.
Lan' guid, faint, heartless.
Lan' guish, to pine away.
Lar'board, the left hand side on board a ship.
Lark, a singing bird.
Laud' a ble, praiseworthy.
Law' ful, agreeably to law.
Lawn, open ground, fine linen
Leaf, part of a book, green part of a plant.
Leap'year, every 4th year.
Learn' er, one yet in his rudi-
ments.
Learn'ing, literature. [imals.
Leath'er, tanned skins of an-
Lec' ture, a discourse on any
Le' gal, lawful. [subject.
Leg er de main', sleight of hand. [read.
Leg'i ble, such as may be
Lei' sure, freedom from busi-
ness. [a lease is given.
Les see', the person to whom
Les sor', one who gives a lease.
Le' ver, a mechanical power, a pole or stick used in mo-
ving heavy bodies.
Lev' i ty, lightness.
Li'bel, a defamatory writing.
Lib er al'i ty, munificence.
Lib' er ty, freedom.
Li' bra ry, a collection of books.
Liège, a sovereign.
Lieu, place, room.

Lieu ten'an cy, the office of a lieutenant.

Life, state of a living crea- [ture.

Life'less, without life.

Lig'a ture, a bandage.

Light fin'ger ed, thievish.

Like'ness, resemblance.

Lin'e age, race, progeny.

Lin'i ment, ointment.

Lin' net, a singing bird.

Liq'uid, fluid.

List'less, careless.

List'less ness, inattention.

Lit' er al, according to the letter.

Lit er a' ti, the learned.

Lit' era ture, learning.

Loathe, to hate.

Loathe'some, abhorred.

Lo ca'tion, situation.

Loft'i ness, height, sublimity.

Log'ic, the art of reasoning.

Loi'ter, to linger.

Lon gev'i ty, length of life.

Lo quac'i ty, too much talk.

Lot'te ry. a game of chance.

Love, kindness, affection.

Lough (lok), a lake. [ness.

Low'li ness, humility, weak-

Loy'al ty, with fidelity.

Luck'y, fortunate.

Lu'cra tive, gainful.

Lu'di crous, burlesque.

Lu'min ous, shining.

Lu'na cy, madness, influenced by the moon.

Lus'cious, sweet, delightful.

Lux u' ri ant, exuberant.

Lux' u ry, voluptuousness.

M.

Ma chine', an engine.

Mack'er el, a sea fish.

Mag'ic, dealing with spirits.

Mag'is trate, a man invested with authority.

Mag'ni fi er, a glass which en- larges the size of objects.

Mag nif' i cent, grand.

Mag'ni tude, greatness.

Ma jes' tic, august, stately.

Main' te nance, support.

Maize, indian corn.

Ma jor' i ty, the greatest number.

Ma lev' o lence, ill will.

Mal' ice, deliberate mischief.

Ma li' cious, intending ill.

Man, the male of the human species. [hands.

Man'a cles, chains for the

Man'age, to conduct, to gov- [ern.

Man'date, a command.

Man'ful ly, boldly, stoutly.

Man'i fest, to show plainly.

Man kind', the human race.

Man œu' vre, (man oo' ver), skill in war.

Man' tua ma ker, one who makes gowns.

Man' u al, a small book.

Man u fac'ture, any thing made by art.

Man'u script, a written book.

Ma rau'der (ma ro'der) a sol- dier that roves about in quest of plunder.

Mar' riage, the union of man and woman for life.

Mar'tyr, one who dies for the truth.

Mas' cu line, male.

Mas'te ry, pre-eminence.

Ma ter'nal, motherly.

Math e mat'ics, science of number and measure.

Ma'tron, an elderly lady.

Ma tu' ri ty, ripeness.

Max'im, a general principle.

Mead, a meadow.

Meas'ure, a rule, quantity.

Me chan'ic, a manufacturer.

Me di a' tor, an intercessor.

Med'i cine, a remedy, physic

Med i ta'tion, contemplation

Mel'an cho ly, gloomy, dismal.

Mel'o dy, harmony.

Mem'o ry, remembrance.

Men'tal, intellectual.

Mer'can tile, commercial.

Mer'cy, tenderness.

Mer'ri ment, mirth, gayety.

Mes'sen ger, one who carries an errand.　[glass.

Mi' cro scope, a magnifying

Mid'dle, equally distant from the extremes.

Mil'dew, a disease in plants.

Mile, 320 rods.

Mi li'tia, (*me lish' ya*) train-bands, national force.

Mind, that which thinks.

Min'er al, a fossil body.

Min'ia ture, representation in small compass. [agent.

Min'is ter, a clergyman, an

Mir'ror, a looking-glass.

Mis'chievous, hurtful, spiteful.

Mi'ser, a covetous wretch.

Mis'e ry, wretchedness.

Mis for'tune, calamity.

Mis'sion a ry, one sent to propagate religion.

Mis take', errour.

Mit i ga'tion, abatement.

Mod'es ty, decency, chastity.

Mod u la'tion, agreeable har-

Moi'e ty, half.　[mony.

Mo'ment, an indivisible particle of time.

Mon'arch, a king.　[week.

Mon' day, second day of the

Mon'u ment, any thing to perpetuate memory.

Morn' ing, first appearance of light.

Mo rose', sour, peevish.

Mort ga gee', he that takes a mortgage.　[mortgage.

Mort' ga ger, he that gives a

Mor'tal, subject to death.

Mo' tive, the reason for action.　[tion.

Moul'der, to waste.

Moun'tain, a large hill.

Moun'te bank, a quack doctor.　[tor.

Mourn'ful, sorrowful,

Mul'ti tude, a great number.

Mu se'um, a repository of curiosities.　[music.

Mu si' cian, one skilled in

Mu'ti ny, insurrection.

Mu'tu al, reciprocal.

Myrrh (*mer*), a kind of gum.

N.

Na'dir, the point under foot.

Name' sake, one of the same name.　[hands.

Nap'kin, a cloth to wipe the

Nar ra'tion, relation, history.

Nar' row, not broad.

Na'sal, belonging to the nose

Na'tion, native.

Na'tion, a distinct people.

Na tiv'i ty, birth.

Nat' u ral, produced by nature.　[thing.

Na'ture, native state of any

Na'vy, a fleet of ships.

Nec' es sa ry, needful, requisite.

Ne ces'si ty, compulsion, want

Ne ga'tion, denial.

Neg'li gence, habit of acting carelessly.

Neg'li gent, heedless.

Ne' gro, a black person.

Neigh bour (*na' bur*) one who lives near another.

Nerve, organ of sensation.

Neth'er most, lowest.

Neu'ter, of neither party.

Night' in gale, a small bird that sings in the night.

Ni'tre, saltpetre.

No'bod y, not any one.

Noc'tur nal, nightly.

Noise, any sound, outcry.

Nom in a'tion, act of naming.

Non'plus, puzzle.

Non'sense, unmeaning language.

North'star, the pole star.

Nose'gay, a bunch of flowers.

No'ta ry, a public officer.

Noth'ing, not any thing.

No'tice, remark, information.

No'tion, thought, opinion.

No to'ri ous, publicly known.

Nov'ice, one uninstructed.

Nour'ish ment, sustenance, food. [sive.

Nui'sance, something offen-

Num'ber, aggregate of units.

Nu'mer ous, containing many

Nup'tial, marriage.

Nu'tri ment, food, aliment.

O.

Ob'du rate, hard of heart.

O be'di ence, submission to authority. [thority.

O be'di ent, submissive to au-

Ob'e lisk, a pyramid, this mark (†). [mission.

O bey (*o ba'*), to pay sub-

O blige', compel.

Ob'long, longer than broad.

Ob scure', dark, abstruse.

Ob se'qui ous, obedient.

Ob ser va'tion, noting re-

Ob'so lete, disused. [mark.

Ob'sti nate, stubborn.

Ob struct', to hinder.

Ob'vi ous, open, plain.

Oc cu pa'tion, trade, vocation.

Oc'cur, to happen.

Oc'ta gon, a figure of eight sides.

Oc ta'vo, a book in which a sheet makes 8 leaves.

Oc'u lar, known by the eye.

O'di ous, hateful.

O'dour, scent, fragrance.

Of fence', crime, injury.

Of fend'er, a transgressor.

Of'fer ing, sacrifice, oblation.

Om'in ous, foreshowing ill.

O mis'sion, neglect of duty.

Om nip'o tence, almighty power. [presence.

Om ni pres'ence, unbounded

Om nis'ci ence, infinite wisdom.

on'ly, singly, simply. [dark.

O paque', not transparent,

O'pi ate, a medicine that causes sleep.

Op po'nent, an antagonist.

Op pose', to resist.

Op pres'sive, cruel, heavy.

Op'tion, choice.

Op'u lent, rich, wealthy.

O'ral, delivered by mouth.

Or'ange, a tropical fruit.

O ra'tion, a rhetorical speech

Or'a tor, a public speaker.

Orb, a circular body. [cree.

Or dain', to appoint, to de-

Or'gan, natural instrument, as the tongue is the organ of speech; a musical instrument.

Or'i fice, any opening.

Or'i gin, beginning.

Or'na ment, embellishment.

Or'phan, one bereft of parents.

Or thog'ra phy, the art or practice of spelling.

Os ten ta'tion, vain show.

O ver come', to subdue.

O ver much', too much.

O ver see', to superintend.

Out'let, passage outwards.

Out'line, a sketch.

Out'rage, open violence.

Out vote', to surpass in votes.

P.

Pa cif'ic, mild, gentle, appeasing.

15

Pad'lock, a hanging lock.

Pa'gan, a heathen.

Page, side of a leaf.

Pain, sensation of uneasiness.

Pain'ful, full of pain.

Pal'ace, a royal house,

Pal' pa ble, gross, easily de-
tected.   [bound.

Pam'phlet, a small book un-

Pan e gyr'ic, a eulogy.

Pan ta loons', a man's garment.

Par'a dise, place of felicity.

Par'a mount, superior.

Par'a sol, a small umbrella.

Pàr'boil, to half boil.

Pàr'don, forgiveness.

Pa rent, a father, or mother.

Pàr' rot, a talking bird.

Pàr'si mo ny, covetousness.

Pàr'son, a clergyman.

Pàr tic'i pate, to partake.

Pàr'ti ci ple, a word partak-
ing of a noun and a verb.

Pàr tic'u lar, regular, odd.

Pàrt'ner, an associate.

Pas'sen ger, a traveller.

Pas'sion, commotion of the
mind.

Pas'time, sport, amusement.

Pas'tor, a clergyman.

Pas'ture, land for grazing.

Pat'ent, exclusive right.

Pa ter' nal, fatherly.

Pa'tience, calmness under
suffering.   [try.

Pa'tri ot, a lover of his coun-

Pat'tern, a specimen.

Pau'per, a poor person.

Pawn, a pledge.

Pay'ment, act of paying.

Peace, quiet, rest.

Peace'ma ker, one who re-
stores peace.

Pe cu'li ar, appropriate.

Pe cu' ni a ry, relating to
money.

Ped'a gogue, a schoolmaster.

Ped'i gree, genealogy.

Ped'ler, a dealer in small
wares.

Peev'ish, petulent.

Pen'al ty, punishment.

Pen'du lum, part of a clock.

Pen'i tent, contrite.

Pen'man, a writer.

Pen'sion, yearly allowance.

Pe nu'ri ous, niggardly.

Pen'u ry, poverty.

Per di'tion, destruction.

Per fid'i ous, treacherous.

Per form', to execute.

Per'fume, sweet odour.

Per'il, danger, hazard.

Per'ju ry, false oath.

Per'ma nent, durable.

Per ni'cious, destructive.

Per pet'u al, never ceasing.

Per plex', to embarrass.

Per'son, a human being.

Per' son al, belonging to a
person.

Pers pi cu'i ty, clearness.

Pe ruse', to read.

Pe ti'tion, request, prayer.

Pet'ty, small.

Phan'tom, a fancied vision.

Pheas'ant, a bird.

Phi'al, a small bottle.

Phra se ol'o gy, style, diction.

Phren sy, madness.

Phthis'ic, shortness of breath.

Phy si cian (*fe zish' an*), one
who professes the art of
healing.

Pierc'ing, penetrating.

Pig'my, a very little person.

Pil'lage, plunder, booty.

Pi'ous, religious.

Pi'ra cy, robbing on the sea.

Pi'rate, a sea robber.

Pis'tol, a hand gun.

Pit'e ous, mournful, tender.

Pit i ful, melancholy.

Plac'id, gentle, quiet.
Plague, pestilence.
Plaid, a checked cloth.
Plant, a vegetable produc-
tion.   [planets.
Plan'e ta ry, pertaining to
Plan ta'tion, a colony.
Pla ton'ic, pure, refined.
Plat ter, a large dish.
Plâu'dit, applause.
Plâu'si ble, specious.
Play, amusement, sport.
Pleas'ant, delightful.
Pleas'an try, merriment.
Pleas'ure, gratification.
Pledge, a pawn.
Plen'a ry, full, complete.
Plen ti ful, abundant.
Pleu'ri sy, a disease.
Pli'a ble, flexible.
Plough, an instrument of
agriculture.
Plough'share, the iron part
of a plough which loosens
the soil.
Plu'mage, feathers.
Plum'met, a leaden weight.
Plun'der, spoils of war.
Plu'ral, more than one.
Pneu mat'ics, doctrine of the
air.   [tion.
Po'em, a metrical composi-
Po'e sy, poetry.   [tion.
Po'et ry, metrical composi-
Poig'nan cy, sharpness, as-
perity.
Poig'nant, sharp, severe.
Poi'son, what destroys life.
Pole, a long stick ; northern
or southern extremity of
the earth.
Po lice (*po leese'*) the regula-
tion and government of a
city or country.
Po lite', elegant of manners.
Po lite'ness, gentility.
Pol lu'tion, defilement.

Pol'i tics, science of govern-
ment.
Po ma'tum, an ointment for
the hair.
Póme'gran ate, a fruit.
Pom'pous, splendid, grand.
Pon'der ous, weighty.
Pon'iard, a dagger.
Pon'tiff, a high priest.
Po'ny, a small horse.
Pop'lar, a tree.
Pop'u lace, the multitude.
Pop u lar'i ty, favour of the
people.   [ried.
Por'ta ble, that may be car-
Por ten'tous, ill-boding.
Port man teau (*pŏrt man'to*)
a bag in which clothes are
carried.   [real life.
Pŏr'trait, picture drawn from
Po si'tion, situation.
Pos'i tive ly, absolutely.
Pos ses'sion, having in one's
own power.   [flood.
Pŏst di lu' vi an, since the
Pŏst haste', great haste.
Pŏst' mas ter, one who has
the charge of a post office.
Pŏst'script, a writing added
to the end of a letter.
Pot'ash, fixed, alkaline salt.
Po'tent, powerful.
Po'ten tate, sovereign.
Pov'er ty, indigence.
Pŏul'try, domestic fowls.
Pow'er, ability, force.
Pow'er ful, mighty, effica-
cious.
Praise, commendation.
Praise' wor THY, commend-
able.
Pray'er, petition, entreaty.
Pre'am ble, introduction.
Pre cede', to go before.
Pre ced'ing, going before.
Pre'cept, a rule.
Pre cep'tor, a teacher.

Prec'i pice, a perpendicular fall.

Pre cis'ion, exact limitation.

Pre dict', to foretell.

Pref'ace, introduction.

Pre ma ture', ripe too soon.

Pre'mi um, reward proposed.

Pre par'a to ry, introductory

Pre pare', to make ready.

Pres'ent, not past, a gift.

Pres'ent ly, soon.

Pres'i dent, one at the head of others.

Pre sume', to suppose.

Pre tend', to allege falsely.

Pre text', pretence.

Pret ty (prit'te) neat, elegant.

Pre vail', to overcome.

Pre ven'tion, hindrance.

Pre'vi ous, antecedent.

Pri'ma ry, first, original.

Prim'er, a book for children.

Prim'rose, a flower.

Prince, son of a king.

Print'er, one who prints.

Pris'on, a jail.

Pris'on er, a captive.

Pri'va cy, secrecy.

Pri va teer', a private ship of war.   [tage.

Priv'i lege, peculiar advan-

Prob'a ble, likely.

Pro'bate, proof of a will.

Prob'i ty, honesty, sincerity.

Prob'lem, a question propo-sed.

Prod'i gal, a spendthrift.

Pro di'gious, amazing, mon-strous.

Prod'uce, product,

Pro duc'tion, fruit, product.

Pro fane', irrevent.

Pro fes'sion, declaration.

Pro fes'sor, a public teacher of some art.   [face.

Pr file, (pro feel') the side

Pfo'it a ble, advantageous.

Prof'li gate, abandoned.

Pro found', deep, learned.

Pro fuse', lavish.

Pro fu'sion, abundance.

Prog'e ny, offspring.

Pro gres'sive, advancing.

Pro hib'it, to forbid.

Pro lif'ic, fruitful.

Pro mis'cu ous, mingled.

Prom'ise, to give one's word.

Prompt'ly, readily.

Prone'ness, inclination.

Pro nounce', to articulate by the organs of speech.

Pro nun ci a'tion, act or mode of utterance.

Prop'er, peculiar, fit.

Pro phet'ic, foretelling.

Pro pi ti ate, (pro pish'e ate) to conciliate.

Pro po'sal, scheme or design.

Prop o si'tion, thing propo-sed.

Pro pri'e ty, accuracy.

Prose, language not restrain-ed by numbers.

Pros'e lyte, a convert.

Pros'per i ty, success.

Pro tect', to defend.

Pro tec'tion, a defence.

Pro tract', to draw out.

Prov'erb, a common saying.

Pro vide', to procure.

Prov'i dence, divine superin-tendence.

Pru'dence, wisdom.

Pru'dent, cautious.

Psalm, a holy song.

Pseu'do, false, counterfeit.

Pub li ca'tion, act of pub-lishing.

Pu'er ile, childish.

Pul'let, a young hen.

Pul'mo na ry, belonging to the lungs.

Pul'ver ize, to reduce to powder.

Pulse, motion of the blood.
Punc'tu al, exact, nice.
Punc'ture, a small hole.
Pun'gent, pricking, acrid.
Pun'ish, to chastise.
Pun' ish ment, infliction for
Pu'pil, a scholar. [crime.
Pur'blind, near sighted.
Pur'chase, to buy for a price.
Pu'ri fy, to make pure.
Pu'ri ty, clearness, chastity.
Pur'pose, intention.
Pur sue', to chase, to pros-
ecute.
Pu'trid, rotten. [ziers.
Put'ty, cement used by gla-

Q.

Quad' rant, a marine instru-
ment. [four feet.
Quad'ru ped,* an animal with
Quad'ru ple,* four fold.
Quag'mire, a shaking marsh.
Quail, a bird.
Qual'i ty,* nature relatively
considered.
Quan'da ry,* difficulty, doubt.
Quan'ti ty,* bulk, part.
Quar'rel,* dispute, contest.
Quar'ter, fourth part.
Quar'to, a book in which a
sheet makes 4 leaves.
Ques'tion, inquiry.
Quick, swift, active.
Quick'sil ver, mercury.
Qui'et, rest, repose.
Quin'tal, 112 pounds.
Quire, 24 sheets of paper.
Quote, to cite an author.

R.

Race, a running match.
Rack'oon, an animal.
Ra'di ant, shining.
Rad'i cal, primitive, original.
Rail'le ry, slight satire.
Rai'ment, clothes, garment.
Rai'sin, a dried grape.

Ram'bler, a rover, a wan-
derer.
Ran'cid, strong scented.
Ran'cor ous, malignant.
Range, to rove at large.
Ra pa' cious, given to plun-
der.
Rap'id, quick, swift. [ness.
Ra pid'i ty, velocity, swift-
Rap'ture, ecstacy, transport.
Ras'cal, a mean fellow.
Rasp'ber ry, a kind of small
Rate, price, tax. [berry.
Ra ti o, (ra' she o) proportion.
Rats'bane, arsenic.
Rav'en ous, voracious.
Raze, to ruin, to destroy.
Ra'zor, knife used in shav-
ing.
Re al'i ty, truth, what is.
Ream, 20 quires of paper.
Rea' son, peculiar attribute
of man, cause, motive,
right.
Re bel'lion, insurrection.
Re bound', to spring back.
Re ceipt', act of receiving.
Re'cent, new, late, fresh.
Re cip'ro cal, mutual.
Rec i ta'tion, rehearsal.
Re claim', to reform.
Rec'og nise, to acknowledge
Rec ol lect', to recover to
memory.
Rec'om pense, compensation
Re course', application for
help.
Rec re a'tion, amusement.
Re cruit',† to repair, to re-
Rec'ti fy, to reform. [place.
Rec'ti tude, uprightness.
Re demp'tion, ransom.
Re duce', to diminish.
Ref'er ence, allusion to, rela-
tion.
Re fine', to purify.

* *a* like *o* short.   † *u* like *o* middle.

15*

Re form', to grow better.

Ref or ma' tion, change in morals. [tion.

Re frain', to keep from ac-

Re fresh'ment, food, rest.

Re gen'er ate, to renew.

Reg'is ter, a list, a record.

Re gret', vexation at something past.

Reg'u lar, agreeable to rule.

Reg u lar'i ty, method.

Re joice', to be glad.

Re lease', to set free.

Re lief', help, succour.

Re luc'tance, unwillingness.

Re mark'a ble, worthy of note

Re mem'ber, to bear in mind.

Re main', to be left.

Rem'nant, residue.

Re mon'strate, to show reasons.

Re morse', anguish of a guilty conscience. [ing.

Ren'dez vôus, place of meet-

Re pent'ance, sorrow for sin.

Re plen'ish, to fill, to stock.

Re ply', to answer.

Re priēve', respite.

Rep re sent'a tive, a substitute in power.

Re proach', censure, shame.

Rep'ro bate, lost to virtue.

Rep'tile, a creeping thing.

Rep u ta'tion, credit, honour.

Re quire', to make necessary

Req'ui site, necessary.

Re sem'blance, likeness.

Res' i dence, place of abode.

Res'i due, remaining part.

Re sist'ance, opposition.

Res o lu' tion, determination.

Re solve', to solve, to dissolve.

Res pect', regard.

Re store', to bring or give back.

Re sound', to sound, to echo.

Res ur rec'tion, rising to life from the grave.

Re tain'ed, kept. [like.

Re tal'i ate, to give like for

Re trac'tion, recantation.

Re treat', to retire.

Re triēve', to recover.

Re turn', act of coming or going back.

Re venge', to avenge.

Rev'en ue, annual income.

Re vere', to venerate. [pect.

Rev' er ence, courtesy, res-

Rev'er end, deserving rever-

Re verse', to repeal. [ence.

Re vi'val, recal from oblivion. [tion.

Rev'o lu tion, returning mo-

Re wârd', recompense.

Rhet'or ic, oratory.

Rheu'ma tism, a painful distemper.

Rhu'barb, a medicinal root.

Rhyme, the correspondence of the last sound of one verse to the last sound or syllable of another.

Rich'es, wealth, money, or possessions.

Rid'dle, a puzzling question

Ri dic'u lous, worthy of laughter.

Right'e ous, honest, virtuous.

Rig'our, severity, strictness.

Ris'i ble, exciting laughter.

Rob'ber, one who takes by force

Ro bust', strong, vigorous.

Ros'in, hardened turpentine

Rouse, to excite to action.

Ru'di ment, first principle.

Ruff'ian, a brutal fellow.

Ru'in ous, destructive.

Rule, precept by which the thoughts or actions are directed.

Ru'mour, flying report.

S.

Sa' cred, devoted to religious uses. [to Heaven.
Sac'ri fice,* any thing offered
Sac'ri lege, robbing a church
Sail'or, a seaman.
Saint, one eminent for piety.
Sal'ad, food of raw herbs.
Sal va'tion, preservation from eternal death.
Sal u ta'tion, a greeting.
Sauc'ti fy, to make holy.
Sa'pi ence, wisdom, knowledge.
Sar'casm, a keen reproach.
Sa ti ate, (sa' she ate) to satisfy. [vice.
Sat' ire, a poem censuring
Sat is fac'tion, recompense.
Sat'yr, a sylvan god.
Sav'age, wild, cruel.
Sâu'cy, pert, insolent.
Sāv'ing, frugal.
Sāv'iour, a Redeemer.
Scab' bard, the sheath of a sword.
Scăl'lion, a small onion.
Scam' per, to run with speed.
Scan'dal, opprobrious censure.
Scan'ty, narrow, small.
Scep'tre, an ensign of royalty
Sched'ule, a little inventory.
Scheme, a plan, design.
Schism (sizm) a separation in the church.
Schol'ar, a disciple, a man of learning.
School' mas ter, one who teaches a school.
Sci'ence, knowledge, art.
Scis'sors, small shears.
Score, twenty.
Scoun'drel, a villain.
Scourge, lash, punishment.
Scrawl, to write unskilfully.

Scream, to cry out.
Scrib' ble, to write without care.
Scrip'ture, the Bible.
Scrive'ner, one who draws contracts. [tious.
Scru'pu lous, doubtful, cautious.
Scru'ti ny, strict inquiry.
Scuf'fle, a confused quarrel.
Sea'man, a sailor, a mariner.
Sea'port, a harbour for ships to lie in. [trade is to sew.
Seam'stress, a woman whose
Sea'son, one of the four parts of the year.
Se'cre sy, privacy.
Sec're ta ry, one who writes for another.
Se cure', easy, safe.
Se cu'ri ty, safety.
Se date', calm, serene.
Sed'en ta ry, inactive.
Se di'tious, factious.
Se duce', to tempt, to mislead
Sed'u lous, assiduous.
Seed'time, the season of sowing. [ing.
Sēiz'ure, act of seizing.
Sel'dom, not often.
Se lect', to choose from.
Se lec'tion, choice made.
Self'ish ness, self-love.
Sel'vage, the edge of cloth.
Sem'i cir cle, a half circle.
Sem'i nal, belonging to seed.
Sem' i na ry, a place of education.
Sem'i vowel, a consonant with an imperfect sound.
Se'ni or, older.
Sense, faculty of perceiving.
Sen si bil'i ty, quickness of sensation.
Sen'su al, carnal, lewd.
Sen'tence, a period in speech.
Sen ten'tious, short, energetic.
Sen'ti ment, thought, opinion.
Sep'a rate, distinct, singly.
Sep a ra'tion, a disunion.

* c in last syllable like z.

Sep'ul cure, a grave, a tomb

Se rene', calm, placid.

Ser'geant, a military officer.

Ser'mon, a religious discourse

Ser'vile, slavish, mean.

Sev'er al, different, many.

Se vere', cruel, painful.

Se ver'i ty, sharpness of punishment.   [church.

Sex'ton, an under officer in a

Shal'low, not deep, trifling.

Shame'ful, disgraceful.

Shame'less, impudent.

Sharp'ness, keenness.

Sheaf, a bundle of grain.

Sheath, a scabbard.

Sheep, the animal that bears

Shelv'ing, sloping.   [wool.

Shep'herd, one who tends sheep.

Short'ly, quickly, briefly.

Shov'el, an instrument to remove dirt.

Shoul'der, part of the body.

Show'er, a fall of rain.

Shrewd, cunning.

Shriek, to scream.

Shrub, a small tree.

Shud'der, to quake.

Shut'tle, a weaver's utensil.

Sice (*size*), number 6 at dice.

Sick'ness, disease, malady.

Sig nif'i cant, expressive.

Sig nif'i ca tion, meaning by word or sign.

Sig'ni fy, to mean, to express

Sil'ver, a white metal.

Sim'i lar, resembling.

Sim'i le, a comparison.

Sin'cere, undissembling.

Sin'ful, unholy, wicked.

Sithe, an instrument for mowing.

Sit'u a tion, position.

Skate, a sliding shoe.

Skep tic, one who pretends to doubt of all thin s.

Skep'ti cism, universal doubt

Sketch, an outline.

Skil'ful, knowing.

Skim'mer, a ladle to take off the scum.

Skir'mish, a slight fight.

Sky, the heavens.

Slack, relaxed, remiss.

Slack'en, to loosen.

Slan'der, false invective.

Slan'der ous, calumnious.

Slave, one deprived of freedom.

Sla've ry, servitude.

Sleep, rest, slumber.

Sleeve, part of a garment.

Slen'der, thin, slight, small.

Slip'per, a kind of shoe.

Sloth, laziness, idleness.

Sloth'ful, sluggish, lazy.

Slug'gard, a lazy fellow.

Slug'gish ly, heavily.

Sluice, a vent for water.

Slum'ber, light sleep.

Smart, sharp, witty.

Smel'ter, one who melts ore.

Smile, a look of pleasure.

Smith, one who works in metals.

Smoth'er, to suffocate.

Smug'gler, one who cheats the revenue.

Snuf'fers, an instrument to crop a candle.

Soap, substance used in washing.

So bri'e ty, seriousness.

So'ci a ble, familiar.

So ci'e ty, community.

Sol'dier, a fighting man.

Sol'emn, awful, grave.

So lil'o quy, a discourse with one's self.

Solve, to clear, to explain.

Son'net, a small poem.

So no'rous, loud, high-sounding.

Sor'cer er, a magician.

Sor'did, covetous.

Sor'row, grief, sadness.

Sor'row ful, mournful, sad.

Sou chong', a kind of tea.

Sôup, a decoction of flesh.

Sóv'er eign, supreme lord.

Space, room.

Spa'cious, wide, extensive.

Span'iel, a dog for sport.

Spàr'kle, to emit sparks.

Spàrk'ling, shining, glittering.

Spe'cies (spe'shez), a sort.

Spe'cious, showy, plausible.

Spec'ta cles, glasses for the
eyes.

Spec'tre, an apparition.

Sphere, a globe.

Spin'et, a small harpsichord.

Spi'ral, curve, winding.

Spire, a steeple.

Spir'it, soul, ghost.

Spite, malice, rancour.

Splen'did, showy, magnificent.

Spon'sor, a surety.

Spon ta'ne ous, voluntarily.

Spôrt'ing, making merry.

Spouse, a husband or wife.

Spright'ly, gay, brisk, lively

Sprin'kle, to scatter in drops

Spu'ri ous, counterfeit.

Squeeze, to press, to crush

Stan'za, a set of verses.

Stàr'board, the right hand
side on board a ship.

Stàr'tle, to fright

Starve, to perish with hunger

Sta'tion er, a seller of paper

Stat'ue, an image

Stat'ure, the height of any
animal.

Stat'ute, a law.

Stead'fast, firm, constant.

Steal't, secret act.

Stee'ple, turret of a church.

Stern'ness, severity of look.

Stig'ma, mark of infamy.

Stim'u late, to excite.

Sting, sharp point, with which
some animals are armed.

Strān'ger, one unknown.

Strat'a gem, an artifice.

Stren'u ous, zealous, vehe-
ment.

Stub'born, obstinate.

Stu'dent, a scholar.

Stu'di ous, given to books.

Stu pen'dous, wonderful.

Stur'dy, hard, stout.

Sub due', to crush, to conquer.

Sub lime', exalted, grand.

Sub mis'sive, humble.

Sub'se quent, following in
train. [living.

Sub sist', to have means of

Subt'le, artful, cunning.

Sub tract', to take away a
part. [order.

Suc ceed'ing, following in

Suc cess'ful, prosperous.

Suc ces'sion, one thing following another.

Suf fice, (suf fize') to be
enough, to satisfy.

Suf fi'cient, enough, compe-
tent.

Su'i cide, self-murder.

Sul'phur, brimstone.

Sul'try, hot and close.

Sum'ma ry, a compendium.

Sum'mer, the second or warm
season. [thority.

Sum'mon, to call with au-

Sump'tu ous, splendid.

Sun'beam, ray of the sun.

Su per'flu ous, exuberant.

Su per in tend', to oversee.

Su per'la tive, expressing the
highest degree.

Su per sede', to set aside.

Sup'pli ant, intreating.

Sup'pli cate, to implore. [ity.
Su preme', highest in author-
Sure ly (*shure' ly*) certainly.
Su r'name, family name.
Su r tôut', a large coat.
Sus pend'ing, stopping, or de-
laying for a time.
Swerve, to deviate.
Swoon, a fainting fit.
Sword, a weapon of war.
Syc'o phant, a flatterer.
Sym'me try, proportion.
Sym' pa thy, fellow feeling.
Symp'tom, a sign, a token.
Sys'tem, a scheme, method.
T.
Tac'it, silent, implied.
Tail' or, one who makes
clothes. [former.
Tale'bear er, an officious in-
Tan'ner, one who tans lea-
Tav'ern, an inn. [ther.
Tâu tol'o gy, repetition.
Teach'er, an instructer.
Te'di ous, wearisome.
Tel'e scope, a glass to view
distant objects.
Tem' per, disposition.
Tem'per ance, moderation.
Tem'pe rate, moderate, sober.
Temp ta'tion, enticement.
Ten'der, easily pained, kind,
soft.
Ten'et, opinion, principle.
Term'ed, named, called.
Ter mi na'tion, limit, end.
Ter res'tri al, earthly.
Tes'ta ment, a will, the Scrip-
Tes'ti fy, to witness. [tures.
Thanks' giv ing, celebration
of mercy.
The ol'o gy, divinity.
The'o ry, system.
There*, in that place.
Think, to imagine, to have
d eas.

* *e* like *a* long.

Thill, the shafts of a wagon.
Thor'ough, complete, perfect.
Thought, act of thinking.
Thresh'old, step under the
door.
Thrift, gain, frugality.
Throng, a crowd. [ger.
Thumb, the short strong fin-
Thun'der, noise in the clouds.
Til'lage, husbandry, plough-
ing.
Tim'or ous, full of fear.
Tip'pler, a drunkard.
Tithe, a tenth part.
Tith'ing man, a petty peace
officer. [smoking.
To bac' co, a plant used in
To geth'er, in company.
Toil, fatigue, to work at.
Toil'some, laborious.
Tol'er a ble, supportable.
Top'ic, head of a discourse.
Tor'ture, pain, anguish.
Tow'er, a fortress, a citadel.
Tract'a ble, manageable.
Traf'fic, commerce, trade.
Trait'or, one who betrays his
trust.
Tran'quil, peaceful.
Tran scribe', to copy.
Trans form', to change from.
Tran'sient, momentary.
Trans pa'rent, clear, pellu-
cid.
Trav'el ler, one on a journey.
Treach'er y, perfidy.
Treas'ure, wealth hoarded.
Treat'ment, usage.
Trip'le, threefold.
Trip'let, three of a kind.
Tri'umph, joy for victory.
Troub'le, disturbance.
Trough, (*tröf*) any long thing
hollowed.
Tru'ant, an absentee from
school. [reality.
Truth, fidelity, exactness,

Tu i tion, (*tu ish'un*) education.

Tur' bid, thick, not clear, muddy.

Tur'bu lent, violent.

Tur'pen tine, the gum of the pine. [ter.

Tu'tor, a teacher, an instruc-

Twain, two.

Twee'zers, nippers.

Twine, strong twisted thread.

Twink'ling, motion of the eye

Tyr'an ny, cruel government.

U.

Ug'li ness, deformity.

Ul'ti mate, the very last.

Um brel'lă, a covering from sun or rain.

U nan'i mous, of one mind.

Un be lief', infidelity.

Un bô'som, to reveal in confidence.

Un cer'tain, doubtful.

Un con cern', indifference.

Un'cle, father or mother's brother.

Un der stand'ing, intellectual powers.

Un du'ti ful, not obedient.

Un e'qual, not even.

Un gen'er ous, not liberal.

Un guàrd'ed, careless.

Un hap'py, miserable.

Un holy, profane, impious.

U'ni form, similar to itself.

U'ni on, concord, conjunc- [tion.

U'ni ty, oneness.

U ni ver'sal, general.

U'ni verse, the general system of things.

Un law'ful, contrary to law.

Un mer'ci ful, cruel.

Un pléas'ant, troublesome.

Un re lent'ing, hard, cruel.

Un ru'ly, turbulent.

Un search'a ble, not to be explored. [cative.

Un so'ci a ble, not communi-

Un spot'ted, immaculate.

Un stĕad'y, variable.

Un thank'ful, ungrateful.

Up braid', to reproach.

Up right'ly, honestly.

Ush'er, an under teacher.

Ut'ter, to speak, to publish.

V.

Va ca'tion, intermission.

Vag'a bond, a vagrant.

Val'iant, stout, brave.

Val'our, personal bravery.

Van'ish, to disappear.

Van'i ty, petty pride, emptiness.

Va'ri a ble, changeable.

Va'ri ed, changed, diversified.

Va'ri e gāt ed, diversified, with colours. [able.

Va'ri ous, different, change-

Veg'e ta ble, any plant.

Ven due', a public sale.

Ve neer', to cover with very thin wood.

Ven'om, poison.

Ven'ture, hazard, chance.

Ve rac'i ty, moral truth.

Ver'bal, spoken, oral.

Ver'dant, green.

Ver'i ly, certainly.

Ver i ty, truth. [spring.

Ver'nal, belonging to the

Ves'ture, garment, robe.

Vi'and, meat dressed.

Vic'tim, a sacrifice.

Vic'to ry, a conquest.

Vig'i lant, watchful.

Vig'our, force, energy.

Vil'lain, a wicked wretch.

Vine'yard, a ground planted with vines.

Vi'o lence, force, injury.

Vir'tue, moral goodness.

Vir'tu ous, morally good.

Vi s ion a ry, imaginary.

Vit i ate (*vish e ate*), to deprave, to spoil.

Vi vac'i ty, sprightliness.
Viv'i fy'ing, making alive.
Vo'cal, uttered by the voice
Voice, sound from the mouth
Vol'ume, a book.
Vo ra'cious, ravenous.
Voy'age, passage by sea.
Vul'gar, mean, common.

W.

Wag'on, a carriage for bur-
Waive, to put off.   [dens.
Wan'der,* to go astray.
Wan'ton,* lascivious.
Wâr, fighting.
Wâr'bling, singing.
Wârmth, gentle beat.
Wârp, thread that crosses
  the filling in cloth.
Wârr'ior, a military man.
Wasp'ish,* peevish, irritable
Watch,* a pocket time
  piece, to observe.
Wà'ter, one of the elements.
Wà'ter mel on, a plant and
  fruit.
Wealth, riches, money.
Weap'on, instrument of of-
Wea'ri some, tedious. [fence.
Weave, to work with a loom
Wed'ding, a marriage.
Wel'fare, happiness, success
Whârf, a place to land goods
Wheat, a kind of grain.
Where,† at what place.
Whim'si cal, capricious.
Whis'per, a low, soft voice.
Whôr'tle ber ry, a kind of
  berry.
Wick'ed ness, moral evil.
Wid'ow, a woman whose
  husband is dead.
Wil'der ness, a desert.
Win'dow, an opening for
  light.   [wind.
Wind'ward, towards the

Wing, the limb of a bird by
  which it flies. [the year.
Win'ter, the cold season of
Wire, metal drawn into slen-
  der threads.   [rightly.
Wis'dom, power of judging
Wise, judging rightly.
Wit, the intellect.   [mony.
Wit'ness, one who gives testi-
Wolf,‡ a wild beast.
Wom'an,‡ the female of the
  human race.
Won'der, amazement.
Wood'bine, the honeysuckle.
Woof, threads crossing the
World, the globe.   [warp.
World'ly, bent upon this
Wôrm, an insect.   [world.
Wôr'ship, religious honour.
Worst'ed,‡ woollen yarn.
Wôr'THy, deserving.
Wran'gle, a quarrel.
Wrãth, anger, fury.
Wreath, a garland.
Wren, a small bird.   [fall.
Wres'tle, to contend for a
Writ'er, one who writes.
Wrong, unjust, errour.

Y.

Yawn, to gape
Yeo'man, a freeholder
Yield, to produce, to resign
Yoke, a bandage on the
  neck.
Yŏn'der, being within view.
Young'ster, a young person.
Youth, the part of life suc-
  ceeding childhood.
Youth'ful, young, vigorous.

Z.   [cause.

Zeal, ardour for a person or
Zeal'ous, ardently passionate.
Ze'nith, the point overhead.
Zeph'yr, the west wind.
Zone, a girdle.

* *a* like *o* short.
† *e* like *a* long.

‡ *o* like *u* middle.